THESE ARE MY RITES

THESE ARE MY RITES

A Brief History of the
Eastern Rites of Christianity

Edward E. Finn, S.J.

THE LITURGICAL PRESS
Collegeville, Minnesota

Library of Congress Cataloging in Publication Data

Finn, Edward E.
   These are my rites.

   Edition of 1961 published under title: A brief history of the Eastern rites.
   1.   Catholic Church – Oriental rites – History.
I.   Title.
BX4710.2.F55   1979   264'.01'5   79-24937
ISBN 0-8146-1058-7

Nihil obstat: Joseph C. Kremer, S.T.L., *Censor deputatus.*
Imprimatur: ✢George H. Speltz, D.D., Bishop of St. Cloud, Minnesota. January 3, 1980.

Contents

Introduction

"Ever since the disastrous events of the year 1054," says Donald Attwater, "the Catholic Church has appeared to the world as something perilously like an institution of purely Western, Latin, European origin and *ethos*,"[1] whereas, in fact, the Catholic Church is none of these. In response, the Catholic Church answers: *These Are My Rites*—the Antiochene Rite, the Alexandrian Rite, the Byzantine Rite, and the Roman Rite. These, along with the fifteen or more variations which have arisen during the course of the history of Christianity, make up the *rites* of the Catholic Church. Among these latter are the Armenian, Chaldean, Coptic, Georgian, Greek, Melkite, Maronite, Bulgarian, Serbian, Rumanian, Russian, Ruthenian, Malabar, Malankara, West Syrian, Ethiopian, Ukrainian, as well as the Ambrosian, Gallican, and Mozarabic Rites. The last three, together with the Roman Rite, simply called the Latin Rite for centuries, make up what are called the *Western* Rites of the Catholic Church, while the others make up the *Eastern* Rites of the Catholic Church.

Not only does the Catholic Church insist that these are all her rites, but adds that each of these rites has a right to exist in the family of Catholicism. In the *Decree on Eastern Catholic Churches* given at

Rome in 1964, the members of Vatican Council II speak out vigorously on this subject: "All Eastern rite members should know and be convinced that they can and should always preserve their lawful liturgical rites and their established way of life."[2]

CCD instructors, as well as teachers of Church history in Catholic high schools and colleges, are painfully aware of how sadly lacking most students are in their awareness of Eastern Rite Catholic Churches. The attitude generally found is that if you are a Catholic, then you go to church as I do, you worship as I do, you do the things in your church that I do in mine. If you do not, then you are not a Catholic. It rarely occurs to a Western Rite Catholic, more specifically to a Roman Rite Catholic, that there are literally millions of true Catholics of whom the above description is, in fact, not true. Roman Rite Catholics tend to equate themselves and no others with "the Catholic Church." They find it difficult to squeeze into their notion of the Catholic Church such groups as Armenian Catholics, Byzantine Catholics, Melkites, none of whom have ever used Latin in their liturgies.[3]

In the final analysis, Emperor Diocletian (284–305), in dividing the cumbersome Roman Empire into manageable administrative units, is responsible for our present terminology. Diocletian's first such division marked off the western part of the Roman Empire from the eastern part. As a consequence, the Christians dwelling in the western part became Western Rite Christians while those in the eastern part became Eastern Rite Christians. Reasons for these differences will be cited later.

A budding interest in the Eastern Rites of the

Catholic Church occurred in 1958 after the death of Pope Pius XII. At that time there appeared among the front-running candidates as successor to this Pope the person of Gregory Peter XV Cardinal Agagianian. Western Rite Catholics not only had trouble pronouncing his name (*ah-gah-JO H N-yun* will do), but also they found it difficult to place his office, that of Patriarch of the Armenians, within the household of the Catholic Church.

A glance at the opening pages of *The Official Catholic Directory* at that time would have assured them that Cardinal Agagianian was, indeed, a legitimate member of the papal household and a Catholic in perfectly good standing, even though, as the many news reports carefully pointed out, he did not offer Mass in the same way or in the same language as had Pope Pius XII.

A further inspection of the *Directory* would have shown that Cardinal Agagianian could have found Armenian Rite churches in six of the United States where he could have offered the Divine Liturgy on altars equipped with the enclosing veils and curtains that are proper to the celebration of the Eucharist in his rite. Also, the cardinal would kneel on a raised platform to distribute Holy Communion under both Species to his congregation as they approached the altar and stood to receive the Eucharist. With the election of Pope John XXIII, interest in Cardinal Agagianian and the Eastern Rites of the Catholic Church waned, though twenty-one of the twenty-six archdioceses in the United States had churches of the various Eastern Rites.

Most of the Eastern Rite Catholic Churches in the United States do not belong to the diocese in which they are geographically located, since the Catholic priests stationed in such Catholic churches are not subject to the jurisdiction of the local Western Rite Catholic bishop. For instance, the pastor of the Ukrainian Byzantine Rite Catholic church in Milwaukee is subject to his own Ukrainian archbishop who resides in Chicago and not to the Western Rite archbishop of Milwaukee.

Is not the Catholic Church the same everywhere? We have heard the question asked a thousand times, always expecting an affirmative reply. But an affirmative answer to this question only tells half the story. The Catholic Church *is* one in her beliefs and her doctrines, but manifests a marvelous diversity in her ritual, her ceremonies, her customs, her language; in short, her *rites* are many. Nor does this situation display mere toleration on the part of the Catholic Church. Listen once more to the Fathers of Vatican II: "The Catholic Church holds in high esteem the institutions of the Eastern Churches, their liturgical rites, ecclesiastical traditions, and Christian way of life . . . ."[4]

Does not this splintering and fracturing of the Church into segments tend to destroy the unity which the Church so firmly professes? Again, we must cling to the mind of the Church as expressed by Vatican II:

That Church, Holy and Catholic, which is the Mystical Body of Christ, is made up of the faithful who are organically united in the Holy Spirit through the same faith, the same sacraments, and the same government and who, combining into various groups held together by a hierarchy, form separate Churches or rites. Between these, there flourishes such an admirable brotherhood that this variety within the Church in no way harms her unity, but rather manifests it. For it is the mind of the Catholic

Church that each individual Church or rite retain its traditions whole and entire, while adjusting its way of life to the various needs of time and place.[5]

Thus, it should be clear that *unity* rather than *uniformity* is what the Church seeks among Christians.

This booklet, originally published in 1961 under the title *Brief History of the Eastern Rites*, now appears in a revised form to show how *catholic* the Catholic Church really is. It was written principally for Catholics of the Western or Roman Rite. The diagrams were drawn by John Maddigan, S.J., of Marquette University.

CHAPTER I

Who Are the Eastern Rite Catholics?

Perhaps the easiest way to learn more about the Eastern Rite Catholics is to attend Mass, or the Sacred Liturgy as they call it, in one of their churches. Plan to attend an Eastern Rite liturgy some Sunday morning with an acquaintance who has already gone through this experience. You can readily learn from your *Catholic Directory* or from any Catholic priest whether your hometown does have any Eastern Rite Catholic church. In fact, your local telephone book yellow pages might prove to be your most available source.

Have no fear about satisfying your Sunday obligation. That will be fulfilled, and amply so, one might add, for the Mass you attend, depending on the liturgical season, may last from one to two hours. Of course, the length of the sermon as well as the number of those receiving Holy Communion will also alter the length of the service. According to canon law, a Catholic may fulfill his obligation by being present at *any* Catholic Rite Mass (Canon 1249: "Legi de audiendo Sacro satisfacit qui Missae adest quocunque ritu celebretur." [He satisfies the law of hearing Mass (see Canon 1248) who is present at Mass celebrated in any Catholic Rite.].

Some parishes and schools have adopted the practice of inviting an Eastern Rite Catholic priest to celebrate the Divine Liturgy according to his own rite but in your church or parish hall or school. While this practice is laudable, still it does not provide the many benefits that arise out of the experience of attending the liturgy in his church surrounded by his congregation.

First Impressions

For example, let us say that you choose to participate in the Divine Liturgy of a Ukrainian Byzantine Rite Catholic church. Perhaps the very first difference you will notice as you enter the church is that no one genuflects; instead, all make a profound bow toward the altar. Genuflection is a Roman custom. It was the way that a Roman approached Caesar. In the East, however, one acknowledged royalty by a profound and reverential bow. Thus, before entering a pew or before taking one's place in the body of the church, one stands before the Blessed Sacrament and professes belief in the real presence of the King of the Universe by making such a gesture of reverence.

Most members of the parish, then, move to a small table, called a *tetrapod* or *analogion*, placed fifteen or twenty feet in front of the altar on which one finds flowers, a crucifix, two candles, as well as an icon of the Blessed Mother or the patron saint of the parish. Reverently, the parishioner kisses the crucifix and the icon.

In Eastern Rite churches it is at or near this

table that all the sacraments are administered. Here infants are baptized, marriages take place, the anointing of the sick is carried out. The altar is reserved for the offering of the Eucharistic Sacrifice and for this alone. These churches do not have side altars. When more than one priest wishes to celebrate Mass, he joins the principal celebrant and concelebrates. This has been the custom of Eastern Rite priests and bishops from time immemorial.

Between the tetrapod and the altar stands an icon screen or iconostasis. This is a partition separating the altar area from the body of the church. Three sets of doors opening into the altar area are used frequently during the services. Thus, when you first enter an Eastern Rite church, you normally do not see the altar, but rather the icon screen which sometimes extends from the floor to the ceiling of the sanctuary, but may be as low as eight or ten feet. On the icon screen are icons or images of Christ, the Blessed Mother, the patron saint of the parish, the Last Supper, the Archangel Michael, or St. John Chrysostom. Some icon screens are rather plain and simple in design, while others are highly ornate.

As you follow your guide to one of the pews, you notice that the men of the parish sit or stand on your right as you face the altar, while the women sit or stand on the left.

The doors of the icon screen are all closed, yet it appears that the liturgy has begun, for one can hear prayers being recited in the sanctuary area. It is at this time that the celebrant, standing at a small table behind the icon screen, prepares the bread and wine that will be used in this liturgy. When he has completed these preparatory prayers, the central doors of the icon screen are opened revealing the altar. When the steeple bells ring, the congregation stands. Strangely garbed acolytes bow reverently as they enter the sanctuary. Their garments are similar to the vestments worn by deacons and subdeacons at a Roman Rite Mass twenty or more years ago.

The principal celebrant in silence incenses the altar, the icons, and finally the congregation. With this ceremony completed, the singing of the Divine Liturgy begins. The language is Old Slavonic, a tongue strange-sounding to our ears. The priest is singing a Church language not used today by any nation of any people in their daily conversation.

From time to time during the lengthy services all attendants behind the icon screen march in solemn procession around the altar. On one occasion this procession takes place just prior to the reading of the gospel. The symbolism of the ceremony is significant. The area behind the icon screen symbolizes God's home. The body of the church symbolizes the home of God's people. When the Book of the Gospels, God's Word, is held aloft by the celebrant and carried in procession around the altar and then out into the body of the church, the faithful reverence the book by kissing it. Symbolically, God's Word comes forth from God's home to circulate among God's people for their sanctification.

For many centuries Western Rite Catholics were accustomed to maintaining an almost tomb-like silence at the moment of the consecration. Today, however, after the changes introduced by Vatican II, these words are recited or sung in a loud and clear tone of voice. Eastern Rite celebrants, on the other hand, have always sung these words aloud, after which, the congregation responds "Amin," expressing their faith and their will to participate in this renewal of Christ's Eucharistic Sacrifice.

At this solemn moment you will witness no genuflection, but rather a profound bow, possibly a complete prostration on the floor before the altar, by the celebrant or celebrants. Nor at this time will you witness an elevation such as occurs in the Roman Rite. Rather, the celebrant elevates both Consecrated Species simultaneously, while holding his arms crossed.

By now you will have noticed that the congregation is singing the entire liturgy without benefit of hymnbooks, missals, or musical accompaniment. Choir practice is unknown since the entire congregation, including the children, knows the words of the entire liturgy by heart. Only a cantor sings from a missal since it is his duty to sing the epistle and the prayers proper to the Mass of this particular day. If you are musically inclined, the singing alone will abundantly reward you for your efforts to take part in this liturgy.

As the congregation takes up the full-volumed singing of the "Our Father" whether in Old Slavonic or, as in many churches today, Ukrainian, you settle back with the pleasant feeling that at last you are on familiar territory. "Thy kingdom come, thy will be done . . . ." You follow the familiar words in your English translation of the Byzantine liturgy. But as you conclude your prayer with your "Amen," the rest of the congregation without a sign of commotion or uneasiness continues . . . "for thine is the kingdom and the power and the glory . . . ," words that the Roman Rite Catholics associated for centuries with Protestant services. While the Roman Rite Mass has only recently added these words to the Lord's Prayer, the Eastern Rite Catholics have never used any other form in their liturgy.

When you prepare to receive Holy Communion, your guide may wish to instruct you briefly on the proper manner followed in this and many other Eastern Rite Catholic churches. Generally, you will receive in a standing position with your arms folded over your breast. The celebrant will be standing on a step above you called a *solea*. With your mouth held wide open and without extending your tongue, you tilt your head far back. Reception of the Eucharist is under both forms. Normally, the consecrated bread is not in a wafer form as in the Roman Rite, but rather in a cube shape. Too, this bread is leavened; consequently, the host must literally be consumed for it will not dissolve in your mouth. With a spoon, the celebrant will lift from the chalice a single cube of the Consecrated Bread that will have been immersed in the Precious Blood. The Consecrated Bread, now moist with the Precious Blood, will be placed on your tongue. Thus, while you do not drink from the chalice, you do receive the Eucharist under both forms.

Later, when your guide informs you that the bread was baked by the wife of the pastor and that one of his sons was serving at the altar and his two daughters were singing in the choir loft, you begin to wonder. Are these people really Catholics? And if they are, can I say any longer that the Eucharistic Sacrifice is offered the same way everywhere in the world?

If by chance you were to follow up your first

venture into Eastern Christianity, you would meet up with more surprises. In most of their churches, you would find no Stations of the Cross, no confessionals, no Benediction of the Blessed Sacrament, no novenas. Devotions such as the saying of the Rosary or the First Fridays are scarcely known. In their liturgical calendar, you would find feast days that you had never heard of before, such as the Falling Asleep of the Blessed Mother, the Commemoration of the Three Holy Bishops, St. Nicholas the Wonderworker, the Sunday of Orthodoxy, the Sunday of the Holy Forefathers, St. Elias the Prophet, and St. Gregory Martyr Demeter. You would, likewise, discover fast days unknown to you and your Roman Rite friends.

DIFFERENT, YET THE SAME

With dozens of questions whirling through your mind, you return to *The Official Catholic Directory* to check the address of this church that you had just visited. There is no doubt about it. This church does claim to be Catholic and there it is listed in the *Directory*. Still, you wonder. How can they be Catholic when they don't do so many things other Catholics do in their liturgical services?

They do not genuflect; they use a strange language; they do not conduct Benediction, nor the Stations of the Cross, nor First Friday devotions. They even appear to make the Sign of the Cross backwards! And apparently their pastor is a true priest, a true Catholic priest, but married legitimately and living publicly with his wife and children in their rectory.

If such contrasts disturb you, then you should

spend some time and effort in trying to understand the elements of our Catholic faith which are essential and distinguish them from those elements which, though significant, are only accidental to our faith and might differ from place to place in various parts of the world.

There must have been some time in your life when, in spite of your effort to live up to the demands of your religious beliefs, in spite of your open and public profession of the faith, others failed to recognize you as a Catholic or refused to acknowledge the sincerity of your beliefs.

When non-Catholics fail to recognize our efforts to live up to the demands of our religious principles, we are apt to be somewhat dismayed. When other Catholics make this same uncharitable judgment in our regard, we suffer a greater indignity. Yet, this is a rather common experience among Catholics of the Eastern Rites. Frequently, their way of practicing their Catholic faith leads many Roman Rite Catholics to look upon their Eastern Rite brothers if not as heretics or schismatics, then, at best, as a group of Catholics simply to be tolerated within the family of Catholics until they fade ultimately into oblivion.

Jesus was not a Roman Catholic, certainly not a Roman Rite Catholic, nor were Joseph and Mary. "Roman" was first joined to "Catholic" to designate a specific body of Christians only in the sixteenth century. It would not be pressing the point too far to speak of Joseph and Mary as Eastern Rite Christians, for they lived their lives in the eastern half of the Roman Empire.

To return to our opening remarks drawn from

the comment made by Donald Attwater, the Catholic Church has, in fact, appeared before the world for almost nine hundred years as though it were of European origin and designed by its very nature to fit into a culture that is thoroughly Western. The truth remains that the Church of Christ is neither of these, since it is designed by its very nature to be catholic, that is, universal, and by no stretch of the imagination can it be said to be European in origin.

During the first three centuries of Christianity, when all the rites as we know them were forming, the ceremonies commonly used throughout the Christian world were largely of Eastern origin. During these centuries, too, the Greek language enjoyed the first position among the languages used by the Church in her ceremonies and in her documents, whereas it remained for the third-century Christians to witness the earliest use of the Latin tongue in the Church ceremonies in Rome and the regions of the Christian world then under Rome's domination.

At present there are many rites in daily use throughout the Catholic Church. Depending on the basis of division, we may count as low as five or as many as nineteen. When we speak of only four basic rites, we are speaking of four families of rites—the Roman, the Antiochene, the Alexandrian, and the Byzantine. In such a division we use the basic rite as the source from which many daughter rites arose. Eastern Rite Catholics living in the United States today number more than one million.

The same Catholic Church exists in all parts of the world. The same truths of the faith are professed by all Catholics of many nationalities and speaking many languages. The same sacrifice of the Mass is offered; the same sacraments are administered. Yet, side by side with this marvelous unity, there exists within the Catholic Church an equally marvelous diversity: a variety of tongues and customs whose very presence testifies eloquently to the universality within the Catholic Church. Unfortunately, this diversity often leads to suspicion, a suspicion that is based on false premises, namely, that unity necessarily implies uniformity.

In the Eastern Rites of the Catholic Church, the Divine Liturgy is offered in many different ways and in a multitude of languages (see Diagram 1, which gives an overview of the various rites and languages used in the Catholic Church). The normal reaction of most Catholics of the Roman Rite to this situation is disbelief followed by a serious question: How did this diversity come about? To find a suitable answer, we must return to the beginnings of Christianity.

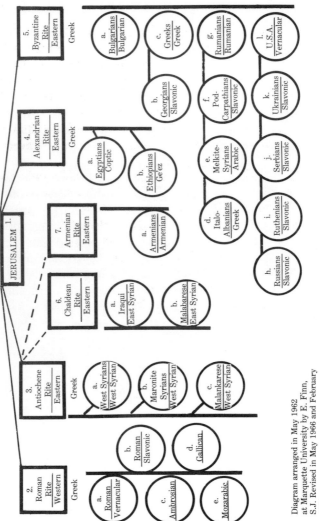

JERUSALEM 1.

2.
Roman
Rite
Western

Greek

a. Roman / Vernacular
b. Roman / Slavonic
c. Ambrosian
d. Gallican
e. Mozarabic

3.
Antiochene
Rite
Eastern

Greek

a. West Syrians / West Syrian
Maronite Syrians / West Syrian
c. Malankarese / West Syrian

6.
Chaldean
Rite
Eastern

a. Iraqui / East Syrian
b. Malabarese / East Syrian

7.
Armenian
Rite
Eastern

a. Armenians / Armenian

4.
Alexandrian
Rite
Eastern

Greek

a. Egyptians / Coptic
b. Ethiopians / Ge'ez

5.
Byzantine
Rite
Eastern

Greek

a. Bulgarians / Bulgarian
b. Georgians / Slavonic
c. Greeks / Greek
d. Italo-Albanians / Greek
e. Melkite-Syrians / Arabic
f. Pod-Carpathians / Slavonic
g. Rumanians / Rumanian
h. Russians / Slavonic
i. Ruthenians / Slavonic
j. Serbians / Slavonic
k. Ukrainians / Slavonic
l. U.S.A. / Vernacular

Diagram arranged in May 1962
at Marquette University by E. Finn,
S.J. Revised in May 1966 and February
1979.

Diagram 1:

– All groups found here are fully incorporated in the society of the Church according to the norms set down in chapter 2 of *Lumen Gentium* of Vatican II.

– Western Rite Catholics are all those groups found under square 2. Included are Roman Rite Catholics using vernacular languages as well as Latin. These are found in circle *a*.
   Included, too, are Roman Rite Catholics using the Slavonic language. This group is sometimes spoken of as belonging to the Slavonic Rite. These are found in circle *b*.
   Ambrosian Rite Catholics who live in the diocese of Milan in Italy are found in circle *c*. They formerly used Latin.
   Gallican Rite Catholics who live in the diocese of Lyons in France are found in circle *d*. They also formerly used Latin.
   Mozarabic Rite Catholics who live in the diocese of Toledo in Spain are found in circle *e*. They also formerly used Latin.

– All groups found under squares 3, 4, 5, 6, and 7 are *Eastern Rite Catholics*. Only those groups found under square 5 are Byzantine Rite Catholics. The *non-Catholic counterpart* to these groups are THE ORTHODOX (e g. Russian Orthodox, Greek Orthodox, and Serbian Orthodox).

– The city of Byzantium, which gave its name to the Byzantine Rite and the Byzantine Empire, was renamed Constantinople after the Emperor Constantine moved the capital from Rome in the West to Byzantium in the East. This city today is called Istanbul.

– In the Catholic Church there are approximately 550 million Christians. About 98 percent of them belong in circle *a* under square 2.

– Each square and each circle represents a group of Catholics that is in some slight way different from every other group of Catholics shown here. The word in the *lower* half of the square or circle gives the language used by that group in their celebration of the liturgy and in the administration of the sacraments. The word in the *upper* half of each square or circle gives the name by which that *rite* is commonly known or the people for whom that *rite* exists.

– When there is a question of a union of Christians or a reunion of separated Christians, there is no question whatever of uniting the Eastern Rite Catholics and the Western Rite Catholics. It is impossible to unite what is already united. All of the groups shown on this diagram fall under the designation "Catholic" inasmuch as all of them are fully incorporated in the society of the Church according to the norms of chapter 2 of *Lumen Gentium* of Vatican II.

– In the United States many of the Byzantine Rite Catholics use English, as well as the language indicated on the diagram, in their liturgy.

How Did the Various Rites Originate?

Let us imagine ourselves in Jerusalem shortly after the ascension. Christianity had just been born. Christ has only recently commissioned certain men to feed his flock. Empowered by their leader, these men are to teach men the truths about man in his relation to God that Jesus had taught. This is what a CREED is: a set of truths that must be accepted and assented to by those who would be his followers.

In addition, Christ had taught in broad outline a set of moral principles and guidelines that had to be adhered to by those who would be identified as his disciples. This is what is meant by a CODE.

Finally, Christ had brought to those who believed in him a new CULT, that is, a new way of worshipping God.

Creed, code, and cult with the person of Jesus as the focal point constitute the principal elements of Christianity.

Christ then directed his followers to preach the Good News of man's salvation from sin and death through oneness with him. They were to go into the whole world bringing wherever they went Christ's creed, Christ's code, and Christ's cult. In a word, they were to bring Christianity to the world. They were to bring men to Christ and Christ to men. Through oneness with Christ, men were to return to the Father.

CREED, CODE, CULT

A *creed* is not difficult to understand. In brief, it is a summary statement of the principal beliefs of one's religion. Likewise, little difficulty is encountered in grasping the meaning of a *code* when used in the religious sense for it simply embraces the principles and guidelines that one uses to direct his moral conduct.

Cult, however, since it involves so many elements, forces us to examine these elements more slowly and with greater care. One of the basic elements involved in a religious cult is that of *sacrifice*. Now sacrifice has many and various meanings, e.g. in married life, in the game of baseball, in religions of old, in the Bible. Historically, the basic idea underlying all of these practices is that of *gift-giving*. In each of the above-cited instances, a gift of some sort is given by one to another. This is a form of sign language. In a sacrifice one person offers a gift which can be seen or felt, offers a gift which in some way is sense perceptible, offers a gift which has shape and size and color in order that through this gift, which can be perceived by the senses, men might express to one another something that cannot be perceived by the senses.

Let us attempt to explain this notion further with an illustration. Consider, for instance, *gratitude*. Gratitude has no shape or size or color. There is no length or breadth or weight to gratitude, such as there is to a piece of metal or a stone. Man does not add to his height when he is grateful. There is no pleasant odor as from a flower or a perfume that emanates from one who is grateful. We cannot taste gratitude as we can a delicate wine.

When a person, then, is grateful, he normally attempts in some way to *express* his gratitude. And the normal way of *expressing* this gratitude is by giving some sort of gift to the one to whom he is grateful. The gift may be one of flowers, a precious stone, some jewelry, some food or drink. The gift, then, carries the message of gratitude. It is significant. The sense-perceptible gift carries with it the interior message of the giver that is not sense perceptible to the one receiving the gift.

From the days of Abraham through the reigns of Saul and David until the time of Jesus of Nazareth, the Jewish people had, under divine direction, been offering gifts to the Lord of the Universe in the form of doves, lambs, heifers, wheat, wine. Usually, such sacrifices were followed by a sacrificial meal. The Jews of old offered such gifts to the Almighty and All Powerful One for all that he had done for them and for mankind. By so expressing their gratitude, they were expressing a very profound truth publicly. They were openly acknowledging God's supremacy and man's total dependence on him for all that they were and all that they possessed.

Against this background, let us consider what Jesus did for all men at the Last Supper and on Calvary. With the simplest words and with remarkably simple actions, as the Byzantine liturgy puts it:

On the night on which he gave himself up for the life of the world, he took bread . . . and having given thanks and blessed and consecrated it, he broke it saying to his disciples and apostles: "Take, eat, This is my Body which is broken for you for the remission of sins . . . ." In like manner the cup, saying: "Drink of this all of you; this is my blood of the New Testament, which is being shed for you and for many for the remission of sins."

Commemorating This Event

At the Last Supper, Christ had through his divine power changed bread and wine into his own Body and Blood and had made a gift of himself to the Father for the remission of sins. He then directed his companions at table, his apostles, to commemorate and renew this sacred event in the years to come by re-presenting the same gift to the Father for the same purpose, using the same signs. With the divine command came the divine power and authority to "Do THIS in memory of me."

For a variety of reasons, but principally because he had so instructed them, the apostles began to move away from Jerusalem and into the neighboring towns and villages. It was to Antioch first that they went carrying the Good News of the Risen Christ. Christ lives. Christ has overcome death. Christ is risen. As they went from city to city and from village to village, they carried with them Christ's *creed*, Christ's *code*, Christ's *cult* (see Diagram 2, which indicates the early spread of Christianity around the Mediterranean Sea).

As new disciples were enlisted in new lands, the same truths regarding man in his relation to God, his Father, were preached; the same principles of conduct that would pervade the lives of Christ's

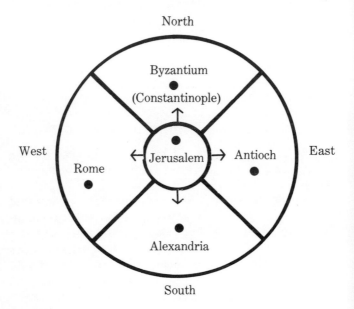

Diagram 2:

With Jerusalem as the point of origin, Christianity spread east to Antioch, south to Alexandria, west to Rome, and north to Byzantium, soon to become Constantinople.

followers were promulgated; the same manner of worshipping the Father through the renewal ceremony of the Last Supper and Calvary was carried out. The same GIFT was given to the Father for man's salvation. Quietly, Christianity had broken into the world bringing the Good News of man's salvation to all the nations.

Within the first three centuries after Christ's ascension to the Father, the Church of Christ was steadily moving along the shipping lanes of the Mediterranean and becoming well established in the big trade centers of the Middle East.

Antioch in Syria, Alexandria in Egypt, Rome— the capital city of the empire, Byzantium on the Bosporus Straits, these metropolitan areas, together with the many small neighboring towns, laid claim to enthusiastic communities of believers in the new religion. Wherever the apostles went—whether to the East, the South, the West, or the North—they brought with them the same creed, the same code, the same cult that had originated in Jerusalem with Jesus of Nazareth Risen, the foundation stone. In brief, they brought with them Christianity, their new way of life.

Difficulties in translating the new beliefs into new languages soon brought accusations of unorthodox teachings. The apostles, and later their successors, had to face the false teachers and correct them.

Similarly, difficulties in applying the new principles of conduct had to be solved so that Christians could be identified as such by the lives that they led. During these years, problems in this area, too, had to be solved by the apostles and by their immediate successors.

As the new cultic ceremony was carried out, minor variations began to appear in the *way* in which Christ's sacrificial offering was renewed. As one travelled from one Christian community to another, he witnessed accidental differences in the *manner* in which the Sacred Gift was given in commemorating Christ's death and resurrection. No one was particularly disturbed by these variations in the cult. We speak of these different *ways* of offering the Body and Blood of Christ as different *rites*, for one of the basic meanings of *rite* is *way* or *manner* of acting.

For example, when the Christians of Antioch in Syria found that because of their large numbers not all could be seated around a table to commemorate the Last Supper, a large room was set aside for this purpose. When this became too small for the gathering of the Christians, the decision was made to move from one's home and into a separate building which would be erected specifically to accommodate the gathering of the believers. Such a building would have to fit into the Syrian environment. It would have to be a place of worship clearly Syrian in style and suited to the needs of the local community.

Again, when ceremonial garments were being made in Alexandria for use by the local bishop in his renewal service of the Eucharist, the material as well as the style of the garment would be clearly Egyptian in character.

Or when a Christian living in Rome wished to show outward respect to the King of Kings in his Eucharistic Presence, he would drop to one knee and bow his head. A Greek Christian, on the other hand, living in Byzantium would show the same reverence to the same King by making a profound bow, bending forward from the hips while making a sweeping gesture of respect with his right hand.

UNITY AMID DIVERSITY

All these Christians, wherever they might be, had exactly the same creed, the same code, the same basic cult, for in essentials they were all at one. Yet, local customs and conventions in dress as well as local languages from the very first days had been introduced into the cult rather freely. Particular practices within the local community, tastes in art, and local styles in architecture had gradually clustered themselves around the essential consecration-communion service which Christ had instituted to serve as a suitable means of commemorating his passion, death, and resurrection.

All these variations were added without disturbing the nature of the fundamental act which all Christians performed in celebrating the Eucharist wherever they lived. In other words, *what* was being done to renew and commemorate Christ's saving event was exactly the same in every sector of the Christian world, though the *way* or the *manner* of performing that action was constantly being subjected to a multitude of accidental changes.

At the Last Supper, when Christ said "This is my Body . . . take and eat," he did not enjoin on his followers the bodily position they were to adopt when partaking of the Eucharist. In his wisdom he left this and countless other minor details undecided, to be determined later by each local community of believers. At present, as a consequence, some Christians kneel to receive the Eucharist while others receive standing. Until recently, Roman Rite Catholics received the Eucharist in the form of a thin, white wafer which the celebrant of the liturgy placed on the recipient's tongue. We should not be surprised to learn that there are Catholics over the world, literally millions, who receive today and have for centuries received the Eucharistic bread in cube-shape. Nor should it surprise us to learn that the cube is cut from a round loaf of leavened rather than unleavened bread.

Should the wine used in the Mass be a red wine? white? sweet? dry? Should the faithful receive under one form only? under both forms? And if the reception of the Eucharist is to be allowed under both forms, how should this be done? Should a cup be used? Should one dip the consecrated bread into the consecrated wine? Should the consecrated wine be drawn through a small tube from the chalice? Should the recipient drink directly from the chalice? All these forms and possibly still others have been used in various Eastern Rites at different periods in the history of the Church.

The matter of language used in the Mass, again, is and has been incidental to the essential offering and renewal of Christ's sacrifice. When Jesus said, "Do this in memory of me," he most probably used the local Aramaic dialect, but he certainly did not add any further injunctions about the use of Latin, for instance. Yet, for centuries, the Roman Rite Mass was restricted to the use of this one language no matter for what Western peoples it was being offered, whether English, Irish, French, Italian, German, Spanish. This practice of imposing the Latin language on all Catholics of the Roman Rite, no matter what their native tongue may have been, has happily disappeared.

Mother Churches

When one considers the spread of the Christian religion over so many lands and amid such diverse peoples, one is not surprised to find after four centuries of growth that there had developed within the framework of the one Church of Christ widely differing sets of customs, especially where cult and ritual were concerned. Specifically, these sets of customs grew up around the four major centers of the Christian Church: Antioch in Syria, Alexandria in Egypt, Rome in Italy, and Byzantium in Asia Minor. In these important cities of the Roman Empire, the four major rites were born, that is, the four major *ways* of carrying out Christ's wish that his salvific death should be commemorated. Named after their point of origin, these rites are called the Antiochene, the Alexandrian, the Roman, and the Byzantine Rites. While each rite differs from the others in many aspects, each has a right to exist within the one Church of Christ. The variations in ceremony and in ritual customs in no way involve variations in doctrines that constitute the one creed. Nor do these ritual variations destroy the unity arising out of the principles of conduct professed by all believers. Each rite has a right to exist and no one rite has a right to reject or condemn or even call into question the practices of another rite.

Like Mother, Like Daughter

From the large trade centers in the Mediterranean countries where small communities of believers had become firmly established, travelling disciples accompanying merchantmen carried the Good News to relatives and friends in neighboring towns and villages. Each brought with him the same creed, the same code, the same basic cult. But, in offering the Eucharistic sacrifice of Christ, each carried with him the local customs, rituals, and ceremonies found in his Mother Church, whether this was Antioch, or Alexandria, Rome, or, later, Byzantium (see Diagram 3).

In ever-widening circles of influence, missionaries from Rome spread through the lands of Europe under Roman domination carrying the Roman Rite into France, Belgium, Spain, Portugal, Germany, England, and Ireland. Eventually, Roman Rite priests accompanied seafarers and discoverers from Spain and Portugal, thus carrying the Roman Rite of the Catholic Church into North, South, and Central America. With the missionaries from France, the words of salvation through Christ came to many of the native Indians of North America, and, again, it was the Roman Rite, as one would expect, that was implanted among the many Indian tribes and nations who dwelt in what today constitutes Canada and the United States.

From Alexandria in northern Egypt, the Church moved south into all of Egypt and into Ethiopia as well; consequently, Christians dwelling in these regions, following the customs of the times, adopted the Alexandrian Rite. Since it was from Antioch in Syria that the countries of the Middle and Far East accepted Christianity, the new believers residing in those countries received the Antiochene Rite for

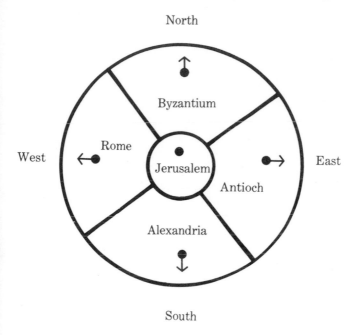

Diagram 3:

The four major centers of Christianity became the launching sites for the evangelization of neighboring regions, eventually reaching beyond the confines of the Roman Empire.

their liturgy. Lastly, from the city of Byzantium, preachers of the Word of Christ brought the Byzantine Rite to those lands in Eastern Europe once known as the Balkans, but now more often spoken of as the Iron Curtain countries, as well as Russia.

MEANING OF RITE

Rite, in the religious sense, implies far more than a mere set of rubrics governing the way one will offer the Mass or administer the sacraments. Rather, rite involves also that whole cast of mind as well as the customs and traditions that a people generates within its culture that best manifests that culture when the worship of God is publicly expressed.

Normally, during centuries of Christian living, a people, whether of Roman, Greek, Syrian, or Egyptian descent, will develop a manner or mode of praising God publicly which fits their particular culture. Though there were times when the Church at Rome suppressed this tendency, still, in our own day, Rome, officially at least, favors such a development. In the East, the Church has always favored these different modes of worship.

It was in the Byzantine area especially that the practice of translating the entire liturgy into the vernacular language prevailed. As new peoples came to receive Christianity in the West, Latin became the predominant language of the liturgy, but in the East the contrary practice of respecting the local language was adopted.

When Roman Rite Catholics in the United States encounter Eastern Rite Catholics, they often look upon the Eastern Rite liturgical practices as strange or foreign, even suspect. To overcome this un-Catholic outlook, Roman Rite Catholics should recall that the Catholic faith came to our shores through the instrumentality of Western European seafarers bringing with them the Roman Rite. If, on the other hand, the North American countries had been discovered by seafaring discoverers from Byzantium accompanied by missionaries from that city, then this book might have been written in an attempt to explain the Roman Rite of the Catholic Church to Byzantine Rite Catholics of the United States.

CHAPTER 3

The Patriarchates and Problems of Doctrine

Another key to an understanding of the different rites which exist within the Catholic Church may be found in the various titles which apply to the pope for the many offices he holds along with that of the Bishop of Rome. The Code of Canon Law for the Western or Roman Rite Church states that the title of patriarch is one of honor only and is a right to certain preferences, but carries with it no special jurisdiction (Canon 271: "Patriarchae aut Primatis titulus praeter praerogativam honoris et ius praecedentiae ad normam can. 280 nullam secumfert specialem jurisdictionem . . .").

The *Catholic Dictionary* describes the many offices of the pope in this fashion: "The Bishop of Rome, the Vicar of Christ, the successor of the Prince of the Apostles, Supreme Pontiff of the Universal Church, Patriarch of the West, Primate of Italy, Archbishop and Metropolitan of the Roman Province, Sovereign of the State of the City of the Vatican."[6]

Pertinent to our examination of the Eastern Rites of the Catholic Church is the title and office of the Bishop of Rome as Patriarch of the West. For too many Roman Rite Catholics this is a little known office of the Bishop of Rome. When we examine the term patriarchate of the West, we find that it refers to that *part* (italics supplied) of the Church governed by the Bishop of Rome by reason of his title of Patriarch of the West. This patriarchate is now more appropriately called the Roman patriarchate, or the patriarchate of the Latin Church, or the patriarchate of the Western Church. The Bishop of Rome is not the only Patriarch *in* the West, but he is the sole Patriarch *of* the West. In the Western Church there do exist other patriarchs, as can be verified by consulting the *Catholic Directory*.[7]

There one counts nine patriarchs not all of whom exercise jurisdiction, but some of whom hold, rather, what are called titular patriarchal positions, e.g., the Patriarch of Venice (recall that Pope John XXIII was Patriarch of Venice prior to his election as pope), the Patriarch of Lisbon, the Patriarch of the East Indies. These three are titular patriarchal sees in which there are no jurisdictional powers. However, the Latin Patriarch of Jerusalem, although holding a titular position, still exercises jurisdiction over Latin Rite or Roman Rite Catholics in the Holy Land.

In the Catholic Church, there are six Eastern Rite patriarchs, all of whom hold positions which entail jurisdictional powers: (1) the Eastern Rite Patriarch of Alexandria who holds jurisdiction over all Coptic Rite Catholics, (2) the Patriarch of Antioch in Syria who holds jurisdiction over all Syriac

Rite Catholics, (3) the Patriarch of Antioch in Syria who holds jurisdiction over all Maronite Rite Catholics, (4) the Patriarch of Antioch in Syria who holds jurisdiction over all Melkite Rite Catholics, (5) the Patriarch of Babylon in Chaldea who holds jurisdiction over all Chaldaean Rite Catholics, (6), and the Patriarch of Cilicia in Armenia who holds jurisdiction over all Armenian Rite Catholics.

According to *The New Catholic Dictionary*, "a patriarch ecclesiastically signifies a "prince of fathers. The title is one of honor only. The patriarch has no special jurisdiction except in virtue of a particular law. He does, however, hold precedence over primates, metropolitans, and bishops."[8]

But whatever name we choose to call it, the Roman patriarchate includes that part of the Catholic Church whose members are bound by the Code of Canon Law, published and promulgated in 1917 under Pope Benedict XV for the Roman Church, or the Western Church, or the Latin Church. Those who are bound to observe this code are Catholics who use the Roman Rite of worship in any of its forms.

Roman Rite Catholics are not accustomed to using the term patriarch when speaking of the pope, yet, he is as we saw earlier the "Patriarch of the West." Now, a patriarch, as the *Catholic Dictionary* informs us, is a bishop who holds the highest rank, after the pope, in the hierarchy of jurisdiction. This definition, it should be carefully noted, is strictly based on a Roman and Western view of the pope's position among the bishops of Christendom. As we have already mentioned, there are many patriarchs in the Catholic Church, though not all of them exercise any jurisdictional power.

Among those who do exercise jurisdictional power over their proper subjects is the Patriarch of the Melkites. When His Beatitude Maximos V Hakim, Patriarch of the Melkites, enacts some law concerning abstinence, for example, for all the Syrians under his jurisdiction, then all Catholics of the Melkite Rite, wherever they may live, are bound to obey such a law. Such a law, however, in no way obliges Catholics of any other rite or any other patriarchate.

Likewise, when the pope enacts any legislation as Patriarch of the West, he is not acting as the Supreme Pontiff or as universal ruler in the Church. In such a capacity he is concerned with matters that concern only Catholics of the Roman Church, of the Latin Church, of the Western Church. Such legislation, for example, would include laws concerning fast and abstinence, the reception of the sacraments, devotional observances, liturgical ritual, and other matters of Church discipline that pertain to those Catholics who observe the Roman Rite. The entire Code of Canon Law emanates from the Bishop of Rome as the Patriarch of the West.

Though Eastern Rite Catholics are occasionally referred to in the Code of Canon Law, the very first canon explicitly points out that the code itself has to do with the Latin Church only. It does not oblige Catholics of the Eastern Rites except in those instances where the very nature of the case makes such an obligation clear (Canon 1: "Licet in Codice iuris canonici Ecclesiae quoque Orientalis disciplina saepe referatur, ipse tamen unam respicit Latinam Ecclesiam, neque Orientalem obligat, nisi de iis aga-

tur quae ex ipsa rei natura etiam Orientalem affi-
ciunt'').

PATRIARCH OF CONSTANTINOPLE,
BISHOP OF NEW ROME

In 330, Constantine the Great, emperor of Rome,
moved the capital and seat of government from the
city of Rome on the Tiber to the small town of Byzantium on the Bosporus. In due time, the emperor
changed the name of the new capital from Byzantium to Constantinople, the city of Constantine. With
Rome's decline in the West as a city of influence was
coupled the steady growth and prestige of Constantinople in the East. This latter city, now the residence of the emperor and his court, became known
as the New Rome. In 381, Byzantium, New Rome,
officially became a patriarchal see.

At this point in the history of the early Church,
there were four notable patriarchal sees: at Antioch,
Alexandria, Rome, and Constantinople. Since these
cities were already important centers of government
in the empire, it was not by accident that they became important centers of government in the Christian Church. As a general policy and by reason of a
natural evolution, the form of government in the
Church adapted itself to the form of government in
the Roman Empire.

EAST–WEST EMPIRE AND EAST–WEST CHURCH

In 290, Diocletian had divided the Roman Empire into two major administrative units which
gradually became the Empire of the West and the
Empire of the East. During these same years, the

Church of Christ became the Church of the West and the Church of the East. Later each major section of the empire was further divided, so that four administrative units, called prefectures, came into being. While the four patriarchates of the Church did not conform precisely to the four prefectures of the empire, the general plan of setting up the structure of the Church still followed the general plan of setting up the structure of the empire.

As a consequence, each patriarchate was built around the foremost city of each of the four regions. Diocletian's line of demarcation ran north and south along the twentieth degree longitude. Today that line would run roughly from Belgrade in Yugoslavia to Bengasi in Libya. The Church adapted her governmental system to that of the State according to what F. Dvornik calls the Principle of Accommodation.[9]

At the Council of Chalcedon in 451, Jerusalem was promoted to the patriarchal rank out of respect for the place of origin of Christianity and not because of the importance of that city in the Roman Empire. In this way the *pentarchy* or "rule of the five" came into being. A glance at a map of the Roman Empire and the Mediterranean area of this period will show that Diocletian's line of demarcation along the twentieth degree longitude accounts for the presence in the eastern part of the empire of four patriarchal sees, while only one rests in the western part, Rome. This geographical situation of the five patriarchates set the stage for the later development of a monarchical form of government for the Church in the West in contrast with a collegial form of government for the Church in the East.

In each of these five cities, Alexandria, Antioch, Byzantium, Rome, and Jerusalem, there was a bishop who was called a patriarch inasmuch as he was the principal bishop of the region. Though each of the five controlled the discipline and administration of the Church in his own region, strictly speaking, he did not exercise jurisdiction over any other bishop in his region, much less over any other patriarch. Each bishop was understood to be equal to each of the other bishops. Each bishop as patriarch was independent of the other patriarchs in the administration of discipline within his region, or patriarchate. Thus, Timothy Ware, a prominent Orthodox historian, observes:

> In the East there were many churches whose foundation went back to the Apostles; there was a strong sense of the equality of all bishops, of the collegial and conciliar nature of the Church. The East acknowledged the Pope as the first Bishop in the Church, but saw him as the first among equals. In the West on the other hand there was only one great See claiming Apostolic foundation–Rome–so that Rome came to be regarded as *the* Apostolic See. The West, while it accepted decisions of ecumenical councils, did not play a very active part in the Councils themselves; the Church was seen less as a college and more as a monarchy— the monarchy of the Pope.[10]

In relating to other bishops, the patriarchs held positions of honor, though among them there was an acknowledged precedence of rank. The Bishop of Rome, that is, the Patriarch of the West, held the first position because originally his was the Imperial City, the first city in importance in the empire, the residence of the emperor. Alexandria in Egypt, the acknowledged cultural capital of the East and the second most important city in the Empire, held second rank. Next in rank in the Empire was Antioch in Syria, which was the second most important city in the East.

When the capital of the empire was moved to Byzantium, that city replaced Alexandria as the second most important city in the empire. When Jerusalem was added to the patriarchal sees at the Council of Chalcedon, the fifth position in the ranking was given to her since she was the least important of the five patriarchal sees in the empire. In general, throughout this period of history, Jerusalem was linked closely with Antioch in administrative authority and in her ritual. Thus, while Rome remained the principal city of the empire in the West, Byzantium, now called Constantinople, became the principal city of the empire in the East "because the emperor resides there." She was the New Rome. Note once more that four of these patriarchal sees were located in the eastern part of the empire, as divided by Diocletian.

THE COUNCIL OF EPHESUS

Early in the fifth century, the preaching of Bishop Nestorius, occupant of the patriarchal see of Constantinople, came under suspicion. He was accused of preaching that though Mary was the Mother of Christ, she was not the Mother of God. In effect, his preaching was a denial of the incarnation, a denial that God had become man and had been born of Mary. According to Nestorius, Mary had borne a child named Jesus in whom God took a special residence.

Cyril of Alexandria saw the grave consequences of such teaching whereby the entire plan of Divine Redemption was destroyed. Because of Cyril's vigorous opposition to this teaching, the bishops of the Church in 431 gathered at the city of Ephesus in Asia Minor for the Third Ecumenical Council.

At this council the bishops established a definitive doctrinal position on the divinity of Christ and the divine maternity of Mary. *Theotokos* became the watchword of the day; Mary was God-bearer—the Mother of God and not merely the mother of a man, Jesus of Nazareth, in whom God dwelt in a special manner. The General Council of Ephesus, under Pope St. Celestine I, condemned the teaching of Nestorius and formulated the correct teaching of the Church. There are two natures in Jesus the Christ, one divine and one human. By reason of his human nature, Jesus is fully man and endowed with truly human powers. By reason of his divine nature, this same Jesus is fully God and endowed with truly divine powers. In this same Jesus there is but one person, the Second Person of the Blessed Trinity. In this one person the two natures are united. Because a woman in bearing a child bears a person and not a nature and because the one person involved in this case is the Second Person of the Blessed Trinity, then Mary is truly the Mother of God—*Theotokos*.

The teaching of Nestorius was branded as heretical and those who adhered to such teaching became heretics or non-believers. This teaching, however, though condemned by a general or ecumenical council of the Church, still spread especially among the Christians of the patriarchates of Antioch and Jerusalem out of respect for Nestorius who had been reared and educated in Antioch. As a result of this false doctrine, the major part of the Antioch-Jerusalem patriarchates was lost to the Church, having separated itself by reason of adhering to a teaching which had been declared false by an ecumenical council (see Diagram 4). The Nestorian Church spread over the Middle East for many centuries, but gradually dwindled to only a few thousand members. One small group of Nestorian believers set up a parish in Yonkers, New York.

Though the Nestorian Church has dwindled away to almost nothing, still, it seems, Nestorianism has not. In the February 27, 1978 issue of *Time* magazine, an article in the religion section concerns recent developments in Christology. The article presents many statements by modern theologians, Catholic and non-Catholic alike. One comes away after reading this article with the uneasy feeling that the remnants of Nestorianism are still with us or that Nestorianism has returned to a new form. "God was present, at work, speaking, acting, definitively revealing himself in Jesus." "The Church should no longer speak of a union of divine and human natures in one pre-existing person." "Christians must discard the 'two natures' approach and speak instead of God's complete presence in the human person, Jesus Christ." "Christians should see Jesus as 'a human being who gradually grew closer to God.' " "It is an absurdity to say that God makes himself into man." Similar statements must have been heard in sermons preached around Antioch during the fifth and sixth centuries.

THE COUNCIL OF CHALCEDON

Within a very short time after the Council of Ephesus, the theological pendulum swung to the other extreme from the Nestorian heresy when the

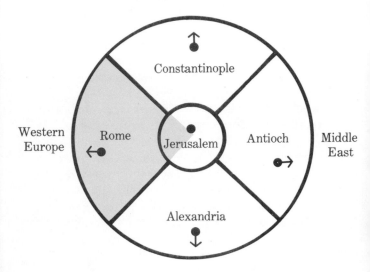

Iron Curtain Countries

Constantinople

Western Europe — Rome — Jerusalem — Antioch — Middle East

Alexandria

Egypt and Ethiopia

Diagram 4:

As a result of the condemnation of Nestorianism at the Council of Ephesus in 431, the patriarchate of Antioch was lost to the believing community. These Christians at this time became heretics.

Monophysite heresy made its appearance in Egypt. Again, this teaching originated in Constantinople, but quickly found its center of activity in Alexandria where the Patriarch Dioscoros gave it his blessing. The strongest proponent of the suspected teaching was Eutyches, a Greek archimandrite.

Where Nestorius had said that if in Christ there are two natures, there must be two persons, Eutyches on the other hand preached that if in Christ there is but one person, as the Council of Ephesus insisted, then there must be but one nature. The community of believers acting through their authoritative representatives, the bishops of the Church gathered in general council, had condemned the error of Nestorius at Ephesus. Now in 451, at the Fourth Ecumenical Council of Chalcedon, after reaffirming the doctrine she had taught at Ephesus that in Christ there are two natures united in but one person, the Church condemned the teaching of Eutyches called Monophysitism or one-nature-ism.

Again, though condemned, the erroneous teaching spread, principally throughout the non-Greek speaking Churches of the East. As a consequence, the Christians of the Alexandrian patriarchate gradually fell away from the community of believers, choosing to reject the authoritative teaching of a general or ecumenical council (see Diagram 5).

Unorthodox Teaching

When one who has professed the Christian faith in its entirety chooses to reject the teaching authority of the Church on any specific point of doctrine, he falls into heresy. The word heresy simply means *choice*. But in its religious connotation, the wrong

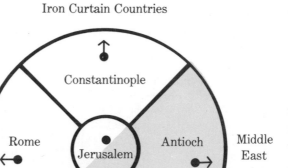

Diagram 5:

As a result of the condemnation of Monophysitism at the Council of Chalcedon in 451, the patriarchate of Alexandria in Egypt was lost to the believing community. These Christians at this time became heretics.

choice in doctrine, deliberately made and clung to, carries with it certain penalties. Specifically, a Christian who chooses to reject a doctrine taught by an ecumenical council becomes a heretic and thereby separates himself from the community of believers. His belief as a consequence is false, heterodox, unorthodox.

Those bishops, priests, and members of the laity of the patriarchate of Alexandria who chose to accept the teaching of Eutyches after it had been condemned as heresy by the Council of Chalcedon in 451 were now outside the community of orthodox believers. In the same way, those bishops, priests, and members of the laity of the Antiochene patriarchate who had chosen in 431 to accept the teaching of Nestorius after it had been condemned at the Council of Ephesus were outside the community of orthodox believers.

In those years, how did one determine whether his beliefs were orthodox? In Greek, the word means "straight" (*orthos*) in "doctrine" (*doxa*). Straight in doctrine or correct in beliefs, these different expressions might well be taken to emphasize the role first of the teacher and second of the one taught. If one believed and taught "what had been handed down from the apostles," he was said to be orthodox in his faith. To determine orthodoxy, a community of believers would compare its profession of faith or its creed with that of other communities of believers. A new bishop on taking office would send a written profession of his faith to his fellow and neighboring bishops so that a comparison might be made to test the orthodoxy of the newly consecrated bishop. Again, a community of believers would manifest their orthodoxy by adhering to a bishop or patriarch who was recognized as orthodox in his beliefs.

At this time, the clearest way to guarantee orthodoxy in one's beliefs was to subscribe to the doctrines proposed by the ecumenical councils: Nicaea in 325, First Constantinople in 381, Ephesus in 431 and Chalcedon in 451. Those who accepted the doctrinal decrees of the Councils of Ephesus and Chalcedon were orthodox in their beliefs about Jesus Christ. Those who rejected these councils were unorthodox in their beliefs about Jesus Christ. As a consequence, these latter designated were declared to be outside the community of orthodox believers.

Orthodox Churches—First Meaning

After these last two ecumenical councils had made their definitive declaration regarding Christ, those Christians who rejected Nestorianism and those Christians who rejected Monophysitism were called Orthodox Christians. To put the matter positively, those Christians who accepted the doctrines decreed by these councils, and the same can be said for doctrine proposed for belief by any ecumenical council, are ORTHODOX in their beliefs.

Since these two heresies arose in the eastern part of the Church and since the councils that condemned these two false teachings were held in that part of the Church, the term orthodox was largely used in the East rather than in the West. Still, one could speak of Christians at this time as "orthodox," whether they resided within the limits of the Byzantine patriarchate in the East or the Roman patriarchate in the West.

Those Eastern Rite Christians who did in fact

call themselves orthodox during the period following these two ecumenical councils were almost exclusively from the Byzantine patriarchate, the patriarchate of Constantinople. Since the liturgical language currently in use there at that time was Greek, it is easy to understand how the designation *Greek Orthodox* first came into being to describe a believer in this patriarchate at this time.

There is no reason to refrain from speaking of the Christians of the Roman patriarchate at this same period as Orthodox since they also accepted the doctrinal teachings of the Councils of Ephesus and Chalcedon. Since Latin was the liturgical language currently in use in the West at that time, it is easy to understand how the term *Latin Orthodox* could have come into being and very probably did, though this latter designation for the Christians of the West who rejected Nestorianism and Monophysitism did not survive.

Caution must be exercised in the use of the term Greek Orthodox, for in the subsequent years the term was applied also to Eastern Rite Christians who did not use Greek in their liturgy.

HERETICAL CLERGY VALIDLY ORDAINED

It is important for us to understand clearly that the heretical teachings of Nestorianism and Monophysitism did *not* in any way deprive the heretical bishops nor the heretical priests of the powers and authority that came with their offices prior to their departure from the community of orthodox believers. An error in faith held by a minister of a sacrament does not of itself invalidate the administration of that sacrament. For example, one who administered baptism while believing firmly that Mary was not in fact the Mother of God would still administer the sacrament validly, and the recipient would be truly baptized. Just as today, one who did not believe in the Immaculate Conception could administer baptism validly. Consequently, unto our very own day, both heretical and non-heretical bishops have been ordaining new priests and consecrating new bishops. Today heretical and non-heretical priests are forgiving sins in the sacrament of penance and are truly offering the Body and Blood of Christ in the Eucharist. This day, Christ is really, truly, and substantially present on the altars and in the tabernacles of heretical churches.

CHAPTER 4

The Patriarchates and Problems of Discipline

PHOTIUS, NINTH-CENTURY PATRIARCH OF CONSTANTINOPLE

After the Councils of Ephesus and Chalcedon, vast defections from the community of Orthodox believers took place in the patriarchates of Antioch, Jerusalem, and Alexandria. The Christians of the patriarchates of Constantinople and of Rome, however, remained firm in their faith. Still, friction between these two centers of the Orthodox Christian world had already made its appearance. Unfortunately, it was friction arising from disputes that would ultimately grow into open rupture between the Church of the East and the Church of the West in the ninth and eleventh centuries.

Had the scholarly and saintly Photius been bishop of any see other than Constantinople, it is possible that his name and his fame might never have been found in Church history books, for he would have been spending himself in scholarly pursuits rather than in Church administration. On the other hand, it is conceivable that his feast day might have been written into the calendar of saints centuries ago, so highly was he esteemed in the East. Not a few admirers of Photius look forward to the day when he will be acclaimed a saint in the universal Church as he already has been in the Greek Orthodox Church. Competent historians have conducted extensive and penetrating research into his life with the result that we are rewriting his page in Church history.

As Patriarch of Constantinople, Photius acquired considerable fame in the East, though Rome and the West looked upon him with great suspicion. The unsettling events of his career as Patriarch of Constantinople play an important role in our understanding of that body of Christians known to Catholics today as the Orthodox Churches.

After Emperor Constantine the Great moved the capital of the empire from Rome to Byzantium in 330, the patriarch of the latter city acquired greater stature than ever before. His power over neighboring bishops gradually increased to the extent that he came to be looked upon as the principal bishop of the Eastern Christian world as the Bishop of Rome was in the Western Christian world. This does not mean that he claimed jurisdiction over all other bishops and patriarchs of the East, but that Church affairs throughout the Eastern Christian world increasingly were falling under his direction. As the Turks conquered more and more lands of the East and as Islam continued to take over areas once held by Christians, the patriarchates of Antioch, Alexandria, and Jerusalem faded into near oblivion*

*A patriarch is the highest prelate in the Orthodox Church. Today there are eight patriarchs in the world: those of Constantinople, Antioch, Jerusalem, Alexandria, Moscow, Serbia, Bulgaria, and Rumania. All bishops are equal with the Ecu-

Since the results of the latest research into this period of Church history are not sharply delineated as yet, one hesitates to explain or even attempt to explain what happened to Photius while he occupied the patriarchal throne. What happened remains something of a mystery. The sequence of events remains unclear. When exactly the major problem arose may remain in doubt for years to come; still, it is no mistake that the trouble which did arise during those disturbed times of Church history continues to divide Catholicism from Orthodoxy today.

"In 857, Photius seized the patriarchate of Constantinople and was excommunicated by the reigning pope in Rome when he refused to restore the patriarchal throne to Ignatius, the rightful claimant." Less than fifty years ago, that statement would not have caused one raised eyebrow among Church historians, particularly in the Western world. Today, however, because of the able research being done by noted historians, principally Francis Dvornik, such a statement would be seriously challenged and in one or other aspect bluntly denied. Did Photius *seize* the patriarchal throne? or was he legitimately *elected* to that position after Ignatius, the former occupant, resigned? Did Photius "take

menical Patriarch of Constantinople, who is considered the "first among equals" (see *Dictionary of Orthodox Theology* [John E. Rexine, 1964], p. 42).

Note the office of patriarch as understood by the Catholic bishops at Vatican II: "By the name Eastern Patriarch is meant the bishop who has jurisdiction over all bishops (including metropolitans), clergy, and people of his own territory or rite, in accordance with the norms of law and without prejudice to the primacy of the Roman Pontiff" (Walter M. Abbott, S.J., ed. *The Documents of Vatican II* [New York: America Press, 1966], p. 377).

over" the control of the local Church by forcing Ignatius into exile? Was Photius "intruded" into the office by pressure groups acting against his will? Did the pope at the time have the *right to intervene* in the internal affairs of another patriarchate? The Church at Rome said then and still says yes, while the Church at Constantinople said then and still says no.

By whatever means it was that Photius came to office, it appears that he was "extruded" from that office by a gathering of bishops calling itself the Eighth Ecumenical Council. Still, upon the death of Ignatius, who had returned from exile, Photius was reelected and was recognized by the Roman pontiff as the rightful occupant. What happened next is again a matter of conjecture today. Did Photius repudiate the so-called Eighth Ecumenical Council of 869? Had that gathering of bishops which deposed Photius really possessed the authority to so act? Was Photius in fact excommunicated by Pope John VIII (872–882)? These are some of the questions that are raised as one attempts to find the right path through the maze of conflicting narratives that have come to us from various historians during the intervening years. Was Ignatius the real usurper and Photius the legitimate patriarch from the very beginning of the dispute? Instead of engineering a revolt against the authority of the Holy See at Rome, was Photius in truth honestly striving to prevent the patriarchal throne in Constantinople from falling into unauthorized hands?

We must constantly keep in mind as we continue this study of the origins of the various rites in the Church that, after the Councils of Ephesus and

Chalcedon, the Church of Constantinople was nothing less than that portion of the entire community of believers that lived in the eastern section of the Roman Empire, differing only in language and in rite from the Church of Rome, the latter being that portion of the entire community of believers that occupied the western section of the Roman Empire.

Members of the believing community whose center was Constantinople professed the same creed, observed the same code, practiced basically the same cult as the Christians of the West and Rome. Because these Eastern Rite Christians had accepted all the doctrinal decrees of the Ecumenical Councils of Ephesus and Chalcedon, they rightly retained the name Orthodox to distinguish themselves from those Eastern Rite Christians who, having rejected the doctrinal decrees of those councils, had thus become heretics and unorthodox in their beliefs.

MICHAEL CAERULARIUS, ELEVENTH-CENTURY PATRIARCH OF CONSTANTINOPLE

Though a permanent split did not take place in the Church during the ninth century because of the Photian-Ignatian dispute, still much harm was done. For the next one hundred and fifty to two hundred years, relations between the Church at Rome and the Church at Constantinople were strained, marked occasionally by outbursts of bitter animosity.

In 1043, Michael Caerularius, Patriarch of Constantinople, accused Pope Leo IX of falling away from the true Christian doctrine and apostolic practices. When in 1054 Leo's efforts to effect a reconciliation proved fruitless, papal legates under the leadership of Cardinal Humberto were commissioned by Pope Leo to serve the documents of excommunication on Michael if he did not retract his accusations. On hearing of Michael's refusal to recant, Humberto carried out his orders by placing the documents of excommunication on the altar in the Church of St. Sophia in Constantinople. Though the canonical validity of this excommunication has been called into question because of the death of Pope Leo before Humberto carried out his mission, there is no dispute that from that time on the two leading Christian communities, Rome and Constantinople, grew more and more distant from one another. A disengagement was underway.

Schism—the Sin of Separation

What took place at this time between the two centers of the Christian community cannot be called heresy since no denial of doctrine was involved. Such a division generally is, or rather was called, a schism or the "sin of separation," as Vatican II words this condition. Moreover, we should carefully note that only Michael and one of his prelates, the bishop of Ochrida, were in fact the objects of the excommunication served by Cardinal Humberto. Eventually, almost the entire Christian East of the patriarchate of Constantinople followed Michael into a situation vis-à-vis the Bishop of Rome which the Western Christian world called schism.

Thus, from the point of view of the Church at Rome, all the Christian East had now separated itself from the community of true believers: the patriarchates of Antioch and Jerusalem by reason of Nestorianism, the patriarchate of Alexandria by reason of Monophysitism after the General Councils of Ephesus and Chalcedon, and now the patriarchate of Constantinople by reason of what, in the mind of Rome, amounted to disobedience to Rome's legitimate authority and resulted in schism (see Diagram 6).

For the sake of clarity and fairness, notice that as far as the Byzantine patriarchate was concerned, the *Roman* patriarchate should be blocked out leaving only the Byzantine Rite Christians as those retaining the beliefs of the community of true believers deriving from apostolic times. In the minds of the Christians of the patriarchate of Constantinople, the Church of Rome had fallen into heresy by claiming universal jurisdiction for the Bishop of Rome over all Christians of whatever rank. This position, so the Byzantines claimed, opposed the teaching and practice of the Church from apostolic times. All bishops were equal. All patriarchs were equal in authority, though from the days of the Council of Nicaea, there was a set order of precedence based on the relative importance of the city in the empire where the patriarch resided.

Prior to 1054, all these Christians of the Eastern patriarchate of Constantinople were members of the community of true believers and in union with the Bishop of Rome or the Patriarch of the West. But, so the Western explanation runs, the East separated herself from the West and as a result fell into schism. The Eastern explanation, to be sure, held and holds to the view that it was the Roman patriarchate that separated herself from the community of true believers whose center was in Constantinople; consequently, the Western patriarchate at this time fell into schism.

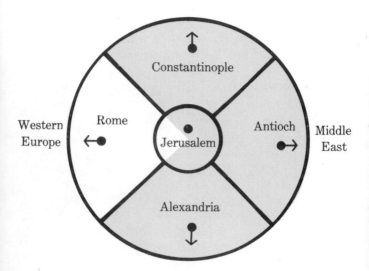

Diagram 6:

Here is illustrated the Christian world after the eleventh century from the Roman point of view. From the point of view of Constantinople and the Orthodox, we should black out the Roman quadrant, rather than that of Constantinople, which would indicate Rome's separation from the Church at Constantinople and from the community of Orthodox believers.

After the separation which began in 1054, these Christians of the Byzantine Rite, though they were separated from union with the Bishop of Rome, still possessed the same *creed* and fundamentally the same *cult* as they had professed before 1054, differing only in rite. Now, however, as the Western Church viewed the matter, a major change had taken place in their *code*. Whereas the Bishop of Rome claimed a primacy of jurisdiction over all Christians, the Bishop of Constantinople and all those Christians who accepted his leadership denied this claim of the Bishop of Rome, granting him only what is called a primacy of honor. The Latin term "primus inter pares" or first among equals is often used by the Orthodox to describe this position of the Bishop of Rome in relation to all other bishops, whether Catholic or Orthodox, whether heretical or schismatic, whether Eastern or Western.

Orthodox historian Timothy Ware makes the stand of the Byzantines at that time very clear:

Now so long as the Pope claimed an absolute power only in the West, Byzantines raised no objections. The Byzantines did not mind if the Western Church was centralized so long as the Papacy did not interfere in the East. The Pope, however, believed his immediate power of jurisdiction extended to the East as well as to the West; and as soon as he tried to enforce this claim within the Eastern Patriarchates trouble was bound to arise. The Greeks assigned the Pope a primacy of honour, but not of universal supremacy which he regarded as his due.[11]

Neither the original act of disobedience, if that is the proper term for Caerularius' action, nor the continued refusal to submit to the supreme authority claimed by the Bishop of Rome produced any changes in the powers of those priests, bishops, or patriarchs in whose opinion such a claim was unfounded. Even though such a claim be fully substantiated, neither schism nor heresy of themselves destroys the powers once obtained through the valid conferral of a sacrament.

For example, a Mass offered by a priest the day before he formally falls into heresy has the same validity as a Mass offered by the same priest the day after he becomes a heretic. So, too, with schism. A Mass offered the day before has the same validity as a Mass offered the day after one has officially become a schismatic. Bishops still retain the power to consecrate new bishops and ordain new priests. Priests continue to possess the power to change bread and wine into the Sacred Body and Precious Blood of the Lord. Nor do those men lose the power to absolve from sins in the sacrament of penance. The separation from the community of believers does not in itself deprive priests, bishops, or patriarchs of the sacred authority they possessed before any separation took place.

It is consoling to remind ourselves that the majority of those Christians who through schism or heresy have become separated from the body of the faithful are not guilty of the formal sin of heresy or the formal sin of separation called schism.

The *Decree on Ecumenism* of Vatican II is very explicit on this subject:

> From her very beginnings there arose in this one and only Church of God certain rifts (cf. 1 Cor. 11:18-19, Gal. 1:6-9, 1 Jn. 2:18-19), which the apostle strongly censures as damnable (cf. 1 Cor. 1:11ff.; 11:22). But in subsequent centuries more widespread disagreements appeared and quite large Communities became separated from full communion with the Catholic Church—developments for which at times men of both sides were to blame. However, one cannot impute the sin of separation to those who at

present are born into these Communities and are instilled therein with Christ's faith.[12]

John XXIII spoke of these Christians as "separated brethren." How many of the faithful at an earlier period in the history of the Church or even today knew or know when their shepherd, whether he be priest, bishop, or patriarch, to whom they were genuinely loyal, was leading them into error or disobedience to legitimate authority? Who can say for sure?

For many centuries it was commonly believed that the year 1054 marked the beginning of what the Western Church calls the Eastern schism, as though within the course of one year the entire body of Byzantine Rite Christians, all loyal subjects of the Patriarch of Constantinople, set up a new Church distinct from the Church of Rome, the Catholic Church. More recent historians of the disengagement tend to stretch this process of separating over two to four centuries. During those centuries the relations between the Church at Rome and the Church at Constantinople were unsettled, but it was not until the fifteenth century, many hundreds of years after Michael Caerularius and Cardinal Humberto had departed this life, that the actual separation became an accepted fact in both communities.

When the two parts of the one Church of Christ became, in fact, two Churches operating independently of one another, is debatable. Competent historians today put the date at 1472, for it was at that time that the Turks, after conquering Constantinople twenty years earlier, had compelled the Patriarch of Constantinople to sever all ecclesial relations with the Bishop of Rome and the West. Henceforth, such ecclesial business as the appointing of new bishops was carried out by each patriarch, that is of Rome and of Constantinople, without conferring with the other or seeking the approval of the other.

A Necessary Distinction: Schism or Heresy

Before moving on in this brief history of Orthodoxy and Catholicism, we would benefit from a closer examination of heresy and schism. Distinguishing clearly between the two will help greatly in understanding the Orthodox.

Let us remind ourselves once more that Christ handed over to the Twelve, those men called the apostles, a divine commission to feed his flock. The Twelve understood that before they all left the scene of their earthly mission, they were to choose successors and empower them to carry on in the same mission of making disciples of all men, teaching them to observe whatever Christ had commanded. The Twelve were chosen to teach the truths that Jesus taught, his creed; to govern the flocks committed to their care, his code; and to bring the Father's love to men through worship and the administration of the sacraments, his cult.

Teaching has to do with the transmission of truth and the communication of knowledge, demanding from the student an assent of mind. When, then, one who has assented and has accepted the Church's *authority to teach in Christ's name* those truths necessary for discipleship and ultimately for salvation, revokes his assent and denies to the commissioned teachers of the believing community their authority to teach, such a one is said to be in heresy. He in effect deliberately chooses to follow an unauthorized teacher of Christian truth. In doing this he sets himself apart from the believing community. He excommunicates himself. Thus it came about that those who rejected the doctrinal teaching of the bishops of the Church gathered in an ecumenical council at Ephesus and at Chalcedon became heretics. They had separated themselves from the believing community. Their faith, their creed, had become UN-orthodox.

On the other hand, the *authority to govern in Christ's name* within the believing community does not involve the communication of truth, but rather the transmission of an order or command. In the first instance, the assent of the mind is principally involved; while in the latter case consent or submission of the will is principally involved. In the former instance, one sets his mind against the one in the authoritative teaching position in the Church and refuses to believe; while in the latter instance one sets his will against the one in the authoritative governing position in the Church and refuses to obey.

When a person who had previously accepted the authority of the Church in matters concerning discipline within the Church or matters concerning principles of morality rejects a command or an order given by legitimate authority, or if he rejects the very authority to command or order members of the believing community, he is said to be in schism. In effect he separates himself from the believing community. Again, he excommunicates himself. Such a one deliberately sets himself outside the community of believers by reason of his disobedience, though his faith may remain intact, that is, orthodox.

ORTHODOX CHURCHES—LATER MEANING

Where schism is the issue, there need not be a rejection of any truths presented for acceptance to the believing community by the teaching authorities within that community. When Patriarch Michael Caerularius and the Orthodox Greek Christians became schismatics in the view of the Western Church, the truths of the faith were the same for both bodies of Christians. The community of believers, both those looking to Rome for guidance and those looking to Constantinople for guidance, were considered ORTHODOX in their beliefs. Consequently, at the time of their separation from the Church at Rome and the Bishop of Rome, the Christians of the patriarchate of Constantinople could still rightfully call themselves Orthodox—the Greek Orthodox Church or Churches. In a word, their doctrine was still straight, ortho-dox, as straight as it had been since the beginnings of Christianity, but particularly as straight as it had been throughout the years of the first seven ecumenical councils.

Still, with the mutual excommunications served on one another by the patriarch of Constantinople and the Patriarch of the West acting through Cardinal Humberto, the designation "Greek Orthodox Church" took on a new meaning.

As we saw earlier, from the fifth century, when the appellation first came into use within the believing community following the Ecumenical Councils of Ephesus and Chalcedon, until the eleventh century, the "Greek Orthodox Church" could be described as embracing all those Christians (a) of the Byzantine Rite, (b) who used Greek in their liturgy, and (c) who accepted the doctrinal decrees of the Councils of Ephesus and Chalcedon.

From the time of Michael Caerularius until 1472, the bonds of union steadily deteriorated in spite of occasional heroic efforts to hold off complete disunion. Consequently, after 1472 an adequate description of the Greek Orthodox Church would have to include a new element which reads as follows: (d) "but now separated from the Church at Rome and the authority of the Bishop of Rome." From the Catholic point of view, this labels the Orthodox Churches and their members as schismatic.

Some Western writers go so far as to point to heretical teachings which must now be added to the position of schismatic, affirming that the rejection of the universal jurisdictional authority claimed by the Bishop of Rome involves a doctrinal as well as a disciplinary element. Here, however, a caution must be observed, for according to the teaching of the Orthodox Churches, a new definition or declaration of doctrine would involve the convocation of another ecumenical council. Since, in their view, no ecumenical council has been legitimately convoked since Second Nicaea in 787, then no new doctrinal declarations or definitions have occurred since that time. We should distinguish, then, between one who positively and deliberately rejects a doctrine now taught by the Church and, on the other hand, one who has never been called upon to accept such a doctrinal teaching. In the author's opinion, non-acceptance better describes today the position of the Orthodox Churches with regard to those doctrinal declarations and definitions which have been made by the Catholic Church since the Seventh Ecumenical Council at Nicaea in 787.

CHAPTER 5

Primacy of Jurisdiction and/or Primacy of Honor

PRIMACY OF JURISDICTION

What really was at the root of the Caerularian separation? Was it the primacy of jurisdiction of the Bishop of Rome over the entire Christian world? Was it in fact a political problem? There is some well-founded doubt about this point. Evidence shows that the Bishop of Rome was at times in fact called upon to pass final judgment when two or more Eastern bishops were at odds. But, we must be careful to note that the intervention of the Bishop of Rome in such a dispute was to be made only at the invitation of the disputants. The Bishop of Rome was never to intervene on his own initiative in such matters, but only under the conditions laid down in canon 3 of the Synod of Sardica in 343. This was a Western Synod and has never been listed among the Ecumenical Councils either by the West or the East. According to this canon, a bishop anywhere in the Christian world is free to appeal to Rome if he is under sentence of condemnation. The pope, if he sees fit, can order a retrial. However, the retrial is not to be conducted by the Bishop of Rome, but by the bishops of the provinces adjacent to the condemned bishop. At times Eastern Rite bishops made use of this canon.

The separation that took place in 1054 was not an overnight affair, but took the form of a gradual disengagement lasting approximately four hundred years. Nonetheless, today members of the Orthodox Churches, particularly the clergy, seem to find in the primacy of the Bishop of Rome and in the question of his infallibility as well, the principal obstacles to union.

Timothy Ware sums up the matter:

> By force of circumstances, the Pope assumed a part which the Greek Patriarchs were not called to play: he became an autocrat, an absolute monarch set up over the Church, issuing commands in a way that few if any Eastern Bishops have ever done, not only to his ecclesiastical subordinates, but also to secular rulers as well. The western Church became centralized to a degree unknown anywhere in the four Patriarchates of the East, except possibly in Egypt. Monarchy in the west; in the east collegiality.[13]

This mentality in the East is reason enough for us to delve further into the circumstances of the separation that did take place whose consequences both Orthodox and Catholic alike experience today. Recall that at the time of Michael Caerularius, there were five patriarchates in the Church of Christ and among them there was an accepted order of ranking: Rome, Constantinople, Alexandria, Antioch, and Jerusalem. The crucial question here is this: Were the principal bishops of these five cities in the Roman Empire who were called patriarchs equal to one another in authority? Or, rather, was one of the five, specifically the Bishop of Rome, who was the Patriarch of the West, superior in authority to the other four? If this were true, then all Christians of whatever rank, including Patriarchs of the East, were subjects of the Bishop of Rome, the Patriarch of the West. Catholics affirm this position of the Bishop of Rome, while the Orthodox reject such a claim, granting to the Bishop of Rome a primacy of honor only.

PRIMACY OF HONOR

If the Bishop of Rome possessed in the universal Church a primacy of honor only, then this would mean that in a procession the pope would be given the position of highest rank, but that if he were to give an order to another patriarch, demanding obedience from him, the pope would be acting beyond his authority. Once more we call on Timothy Ware to explain the Orthodox position clearly:

> . . . Orthodox believe that among the five Patriarchs, a special place belongs to the Pope. The Orthodox Church does not accept the doctrine of Papal authority set forth in the decrees of the Vatican Council of 1870 and taught today by the Roman Catholic Church; but at the same time Orthodoxy does not deny to the Holy and Apostolic See of Rome a *primacy of honor*, together with the right (under certain conditions) to hear appeals from all parts of Christendom.
>
> Note that we have used the word primacy, not supremacy. Orthodox regard the Pope as the Bishop who "presides in love," to use a phrase of St. Augustine: Rome's mistake—so Orthodox believe—has been to turn this primacy or "presidency of love" into a supremacy of external power and jurisdiction.[14]

The authors of the Dutch Catechism appear to be taking much the same stance as the Orthodox where there is question of the role of the bishops and patriarchs in the Church:

> Those who represent the Lord by holding office in the Church are men set free to be ready to serve with all their might. Many statements of the New Testament which tell us that the pastors of the Church are not like the kings of nations, but servants. . . .
>
> Jesus was "as one who served" among his apostles, and at the same time was the authority at the center of the little flock. In the same way, he gave his apostles the charge of being servants of God's people and at the same time his own authoritative representatives.
>
> The fullness of pastoral power and authority is given to the bishops. They are THE priests of the Church. . . . The bishops, as were the Apostles before them, are given authority to feed the flock of Christ by governing it, teaching it, distributing the sacraments to it. This is their service.[15]

A prevalent view today regarding Michael's so-called schism is that it must be judged in relation to the beliefs of the Byzantine Church at that time regarding the pope's primacy. Did Michael believe that the pope had a primacy of jurisdiction in the universal Church? Did anybody in the East hold such a position? Did Michael, rather, believe that the primacy to be attributed to the Bishop of Rome was one of honor only? Timothy Ware leaves no doubt about this: "But as with Patriarchs, so with the Pope: the primacy assigned to Rome does not overthrow the essential equality of all bishops. The Pope is the First Bishop in the world—but he *is first among equals*" (italics his).[16]

If the position cited by Ware for all the Orthodox was the one accepted by Michael Caerularius when he was confronted by Cardinal Humberto's ultimatum, then he could not have been guilty of formal schism. He could scarcely have been formally guilty of disobeying one to whom in all honesty he did not believe obedience was due. To be formally guilty of the sin of separation, Michael would have had to believe and would have had to accept as a doctrine of the Church that primacy of jurisdiction as well as primacy of honor was rightfully due the Bishop of Rome.

To bring the matter up to date, let us examine the position publicly expressed by the present Patriarch of Constantinople. His All-Holiness, Patriarch Demetrios I, in his discourse on the occasion of his elevation to the patriarchal throne on July 25, 1972, succeeding the recently deceased Patriarch Athenagoras I, reaffirmed the traditional position of the Orthodox Churches regarding the function of the patriarchal office as well as the relation of the Patriarch of the West toward the Patriarch of Constantinople:

> From such an Ecumenical See (Constantinople) a See of service, we greet their holinesses and beatitudes, the heads of the local autonomous and autocephalous Orthodox Churches, the Patriarchs, Archbishops, and Metropolitans, and we extend to them a sign of love, peace, and communion in Holy Orthodoxy, and we assure them that our collaboration with them will be genuine, upright, and worthy of Orthodoxy.

> From this Ecumenical See, that of the first among equals of the Holy Orthodox Church, we greet His Holiness, Paul VI, Pope of Rome and first among equals in the entire Church of Christ, eldest venerable brother, Bishop of the eldest Church, and Patriarch of the West.[17]

The problem as we have stated it is somewhat oversimplified and, therefore, in danger of being misunderstood. The political and military aspects of the Caerularian incident greatly complicate the entire affair. There was much more involved than having an ordinary command disobeyed. However, in so brief a treatment of the problem, we must focus quickly on that element that traditionally has been looked upon as principally responsible for the separation that ensued. Restated from the patriarchal point of view, the problem comes down to this: were the five patriarchs of the pentarchy equal in authority within their separate patriarchal sees? Was the authority of each of the five equal to the authority of each of the others when each was acting *as patriarch*?

Stating the question this way forces us to restate the problem regarding the primacy of the Bishop of Rome in his relations with the other patriarchs. Is primacy of jurisdiction over the entire Church of Christ to be acknowledged as the prerogative of the one who is Patriarch of the West when he is acting in his capacity as patriarch? If the Bishop of Rome when acting as Patriarch of the West exercised primacy of jurisdiction over the other four major patriarchs, then the five patriarchs are obviously not equal as patriarchs when acting within their own patriarchal sees. Rather, the situation is opposed to the relationship as Patriarch Demetrios stated it: "The Bishop of Rome, the Patriarch of the West, is first among equals in the entire Church of Christ, just as I am first among equals in the Orthodox Churches."

If the relationship of patriarch to patriarch is understood in this manner, as Patriarch Demetrios understands it, then it would be possible for the Patriarch of the West, the Bishop of Rome, to meet any of the other Patriarchs of the East as an equal, though at such a meeting certain signs of superiority and honor would be willingly granted the Bishop of Rome by the Patriarchs of the East.

As a Catholic sees this situation, the person who is pope operates within three distinguishable areas of authority. He wears, so to speak, three crowns, signified by the tiara. Each crown signifies authority in a different area: (a) as pope, he exercises supreme and universal jurisdiction over the entire Christian world; (b) as Patriarch of the West, the same person exercises a limited jurisdiction over the Church in the West; (c) while as Bishop of Rome, his jurisdiction is still more limited in scope.

By this we mean that as bishop of the diocese of Rome, the man who is pope and Patriarch of the West can enact legislation which affects only those of his subjects who reside in the territorial limits of the bishopric of Rome. Such legislation might also extend to other Catholics while they reside in the territorial limits of the bishopric of Rome. Such legislation might, for instance, include any disciplinary matters coming from a synod of the diocese of Rome as was the case not too many years ago when the clergy of that diocese were forbidden to own rooming houses.

The same person, the pope, when acting as Patriarch of the West, has wider but still a limited jurisdiction. An example of his authority exercised in this larger area would be the promulgation of the Code of Canon Law in 1918. According to the very first canon, the code does not affect or demand the obedience of Eastern Rite Catholics, except in rare instances. Here the pope's jurisdiction extends beyond the boundaries of the diocese of Rome and reaches into all the dioceses of the Western Church, yet it leaves untouched all *Catholics* of the Eastern Rites. At the time of Michael Caerularius, this last sentence would have read somewhat as follows: Here the pope's jurisdiction would extend beyond the boundaries of the diocese of Rome and reach into the entire Western Christian world, yet leave untouched all *Christians* of the Eastern Rite.

Whether Michael Caerularius and his first followers actually denied primacy of jurisdiction over the entire Christian world to the Bishop of Rome or whether he was saying by his disobedience that no patriarch has the right to intervene in the internal affairs of another patriarchate is moot. The point of fact is that the incident contributed to the ever-widening gap between the Church at Rome and the Church at Constantinople.

Just who excommunicated whom? Walter Abbot, S.J., in his notes commenting on the *Decree on Ecumenism*, carefully sifts fact from fiction:

> Neither the See of Rome nor that of Constantinople anathematized each other's followers; the excommunications were personal. By a sad and muddled interpretation of history, however, partisans of East and West focused on this event as marking the moment of definitive schism. . . .
>
> Just before the close of Vatican Council II, Pope Paul and Patriarch Athenagoras made deeply Christian gestures of reconciliation. On Dec. 7, 1965, in solemn ceremonies at St. Peter's and at the Patriarch's cathedral in Istanbul, the nine-century-old anathemas were nullified and the way dramatically opened for accepting the breath of the Holy Spirit.[18]

DEFINITIVE SEPARATION

The year 1054, when the excommunication by Pope Leo IX was served by Cardinal Humberto on Patriarch Michael Caerularius, reputedly marks the beginning of the major split between Eastern and

Western Christians. Short-lived reunions between the Church at Rome and the Church at Constantinople took place in 1274 at the Council of Lyons and again in 1439 at the Council of Florence. Recall that the Orthodox Churches today do not look upon either of these gatherings of bishops and theologians as ecumenical councils. In truth, "reunion" is hardly the right word to use when describing what took place at Lyons and Florence, for neither the Church at Rome nor the Church at Constantinople considered herself to be totally independent of the other. As late as the fifteenth century, in spite of mutually unfriendly and even antagonistic attitudes, both Rome and Constantinople thought of themselves as two parts of the one true Church, rather than as two distinct Churches. Both Lyons and Florence are seen now as valiant but unsuccessful efforts on the part of men of goodwill on both sides to hold together the two parts of the rapidly dividing Church.

In 1453, Constantinople fell to the Turks. Within the next twenty years, the Church at Constantinople under pressure from the conquering Turks formally rejected the "union" effected at Florence. In the opinion of some competent Church historians, the year 1472 rather than 1054 accurately marks the beginning of the Great Schism since from this time forward each Church operated independently of the other.

In the *Guidelines for The Orthodox in Ecumenical Relations*, published by the Standing Conference of Canonical Orthodox Bishops in America, Fr. Leonidas Contos expresses this interesting view:

> It is central to our faith that Christ is not divided; and this conviction has led modern theology increasingly to the corollary conviction that whatever the appearance of

things, the Church cannot be divided since it is the Body of Christ. In spite of the very obvious divisions it is one, though with a one-ness that we may not always or readily apprehend.[19]

CHAPTER 6

The Orthodox Churches Today

We would more precisely describe Orthodoxy today if we were to speak of the Orthodox Churches, since there is no single group of Christians known as THE Orthodox Church unified under one bishop corresponding to THE Catholic Church governed by the Bishop of Rome. Rather, we find in Orthodoxy a federation of semi-autonomous Churches or independent groups of Churches held together principally by the faith they profess rather than by a centralized form of government as is the case in the Catholic Church.

Fr. John Meyendorff, a scholarly theologian and Church historian at St. Vladimir's Russian Orthodox Seminary in Crestwood, New York, describes the structure within the Orthodox Churches as follows:

> The Orthodox Church is at present a decentralized organization, based partly on centuries old tradition going back to the ancient Oriental patriarchates and partly on more modern conditions. It consists of a number of local or national churches, all enjoying "autocephalous status," that is to say possessing the right to choose their own heads, the bishops.
>
> Bound together by observance of a common canonical

tradition, these churches give expression to their common faith by holding general councils from time to time as the need arises.

The relations of these autocephalous churches with each other are determined by a kind of hierarchy of honor, headed by the ecumenical patriarch of Constantinople as the "primus inter pares." The order of precedence among three other Oriental patriarchates (Alexandria, Antioch, Jerusalem) was fixed in the fifth century. "Other autocephalous Churches" are assigned a place in accordance with the date when they became ecclesiastically independent.[20]

In 1589, the Russian Orthodox Churches, with the reluctant consent of the Patriarch of Constantinople, declared their independence and set up another patriarchate centered in Moscow, holding the fifth rank among Orthodox patriarchates. From that time until the present day, this new patriarchate has been known among the Russian Orthodox as "the Third Rome," thus taking on itself the task of protecting the Orthodox faith in place of Constantinople, which had been known throughout the Orthodox world as "the Second Rome." This is by no means an empty title, but one laden with religious and political significance, especially when one considers the relationship between the Moscow patriarchate and the leaders of the Soviet Union.[21]

Over the world today, the members of the Orthodox Churches, now numbering over two hundred million, are found belonging to one or other of the following bodies of Christians: (a) the ecumenical patriarchate of Constantinople; (b) the patriarchates of Alexandria, Antioch, Jerusalem, Moscow, Belgrade in Yugoslavia, Bucharest in Rumania, and Sophia in Bulgaria; (c) the autocephalous Churches of Cyprus, Greece, Georgia, Poland, Albania, Czech-

oslovakia, and Mt. Sinai; (d) the autonomous
Churches of Finland, Latvia, and Lithuania; (e) the
Orthodox Missions; (f) the Orthodox Church of
Western Europe, more commonly known as the
Russian Church in Exile; (g) the Orthodox Church
of America, formerly known as the "Metropolia."
These last two groups, however, are held to be in
schism, according to the Patriarch of Moscow.[22]

We should note that these various groups just
mentioned do not include any of the Nestorian
Churches nor the Monophysite Churches. These last
named bodies, though belonging to the Eastern Rite
Churches, did not originate from the Byzantine
patriarchate. While Christian, they are non-Catholic
and stem from the patriarchates of Antioch and
Alexandria respectively, following the Councils of
Ephesus and Chalcedon. Normally, when the word
"orthodox" appears in the official title of a Church,
the implication is that the Church so named has its
roots in the ancient patriarchate of Byzantium. For
example, we properly speak of the "Greek Orthodox
Church" or the "Serbian Orthodox Church," both
of which are Christian Churches of the Byzantine
Rite. However, the Coptic Church, the Jacobite
Church, and the Armenian Church are all Eastern
Rite and all Christian Churches which did not grow
out of the patriarchate of Byzantium.

The Orthodox, as the title is used today, embraces those millions of Christians of the Byzantine
Rite who accepted the leadership of the Patriarch
of Constantinople and his fellow patriarchs over the
past nine hundred years. In the eyes of most Catholics, they appear to be in schism, and possibly, in
heresy as well. Still, Vatican II says that "all those

justified by faith through baptism are incorporated into Christ. They therefore have a right to be honored by the title of Christian, and are properly regarded as brothers in the Lord by the sons of the Catholic Church."[23]

On the other hand, most Catholics would be surprised to learn that as far as the Orthodox are concerned, it was the Bishop of Rome, the Patriarch of the West, and all those Christians of the Western Rite who followed Rome's leadership that are in schism and, possibly in heresy also, by separating themselves from the Eastern patriarchs and by claiming for the Bishop of Rome universal jurisdiction over all Christians, including all other bishops and patriarchs.

Gradually and as a consequence of this East-West estrangement, the Catholic Church did, as Attwater observes, appear before the world as something perilously "like an institution of purely Latin, Western, and European origin." It should be clear by now to the reader how misleading this view is. These words might well be used to describe the ROMAN Catholic Church or the Church of Christ at Rome, but hardly fit the Church of Christ or the Christian Church (see Diagram 7).

Thinking with the Church

"Thinking with the Church" was so close to the heart of St. Ignatius Loyola that he set up a body of rules that "should be observed to foster the true attitude of mind we ought to have in the Church militant."[24] One who wishes to conform his thinking to the mind of the Church must first surely learn that mind and then follow it. In so acting he knows

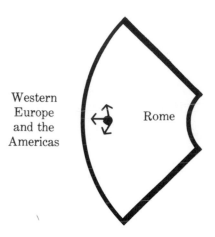

Western
Europe
and the
Americas

Rome

Diagram 7:

Here is illustrated the Church at Rome after the separation from the Church at Constantinople, from the Church at Alexandria, from the Church at Antioch, and from the Church at Jerusalem. The Catholic Church, says Donald Attwater, appears to the world as something perilously like an institution of purely Western, Latin, European origin and *ethos*.

that the Church reflects the mind of Christ and that from Christ we learn the mind of the Father. Christ prayed for unity—"that they may all be one; even as thou, Father, art in me, and I in thee . . ." (Jn. 17:21). Christ's prayer was never for uniformity, nor has uniformity been characteristic of the Church in her manner of worship since the earliest years. The many rites of the Church reflect the many cultures she has touched and witness to her universality.

The Church, ever faithful to the mind of her Master, echoes today the mind of Christ as expressed in his priestly prayer at the Last Supper when in the recently promulgated Code of Canon Law for Oriental Churches, she spoke: "Religiously, let the oriental Rites be preserved, for by their venerable antiquity they not only add to the beauty of the spouse of Christ, but also attest to her divine oneness in the Catholic Faith" (Canon 1, title 1).

Unity of faith? Yes! Unity in principles of morality? Again, a resounding yes! Unity without uniformity in her rites? By all means! These are my rites, says the Church; let them always exercise their right to exist in the one, holy, catholic, and apostolic Church.

When ecumenists speak of a recovery of oneness among the followers of Christ, they are not alluding to Eastern Rite Catholics becoming Western Rite Catholics, i.e. Roman Catholics; rather they are speaking of a recovery of oneness between Catholics, whether of the Eastern or the Western Rites, with non-Catholic Christians of both Eastern and Western Rites (see Diagram 8).

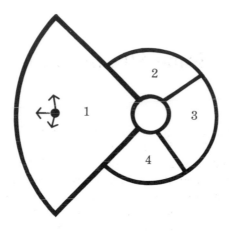

Diagram 8:

The above illustrates the Church at Rome after reestablishing oneness with small groups of Byzantine Rite Christians, Antiochene Rite Christians, and Alexandrian Rite Christians. The Catholic Church today includes nearly 600 million Roman Rite Western Rite Catholics (#1), nearly 9 million Byzantine Rite Eastern Rite Catholics (#2), over 1.5 million Antiochene Rite Eastern Rite Catholics (#3), and over 100,000 Alexandrian Rite Eastern Rite Catholics (#4).

CHAPTER 7

Some Striking Differences

In the Eastern Rites, infants, especially during the weeks following their baptism, which is done by immersion, customarily receive the Eucharist under the appearance of consecrated wine. At the time of their baptism, the infants also receive the sacraments of confirmation and the Eucharist.

In the reception of the Eucharist by adults, there are time-honored differences between the Eastern and the Western Rites. In the West daily reception of the Eucharist is not only common but is also encouraged, while in the East the custom over many centuries has been to receive the Eucharist only three or four times a year. In part, this difference is accounted for in that a very rigorous fast is entailed, sometimes lasting for more than two days and in some instances involving fasting from tobacco and from intercourse with one's spouse.

The sacrament of penance also is received in a different manner in the East than in the West. In Eastern Rite churches the priest usually stands before the icon screen prior to the Sunday liturgy while members of his congregation who wish to receive the sacrament approach in the view of the entire congregation. Without going into detail regarding number and kind of sin, the penitent very briefly confesses his sins and expresses his sorrow. He receives a penance and absolution. There is no enclosed confessional; the entire ceremony takes place before the icon screen in full view of the congregation.

One more word regarding the reception of the Eucharist. Until very recently, the Western Church distributed the Eucharist under one form only, that is, bread. The Eastern Churches have always received the Eucharist under both forms, that is, bread and wine. In the West reception of the Eucharist under both forms has become more common since Vatican II.

Let us remind ourselves once more that Christ left his Church no explicit instructions regarding the manner of receiving the Eucharist. The Church, combining unity with diversity, has not compelled her members to adopt a uniform method of receiving the Eucharist, leaving the details to the local custom suited best to the people involved.

"Utraquism" is a word rarely heard these days among the faithful whether of Eastern or Western Rite. Yet, at one time in the history of the Church in the West, it was a term advocating a much debated doctrine which the Church ultimately condemned. This false doctrine was first introduced by a certain Jacob of Mies who taught in 1414 that in order for a Christian to receive the *whole* Christ, he must receive the Eucharist under both species (*uter* is the Latin word for both). John Hus, a student of Jacob at the University of Prague, later officially proposed the Utraquis doctrine as necessary for salvation. These erroneous views were condemned first at the Council of Constance (1414–1418) and again at the Council of Trent (1545–1563).

Until the twelfth century, the custom in the Church, both in the East and in the West, was to distribute the Eucharist under both species. During these same centuries, distribution of the Eucharist under one species, that of bread, was restricted in the West to Communion for the sick. The change in practice to reception of the Eucharist under one species for the faithful generally and not just for the sick took place gradually in the West between the twelfth and fourteenth centuries, the very years when the gap was constantly increasing between the Church at Rome and the Church at Constantinople. As one consequence of this widening separation, it is scarcely surprising that a change in the practice of the administration of a sacrament in the West would not be followed in the East.

In some Eastern Rite churches, pussy willow branches are used in place of palms on Palm Sunday. Many Churches have no pews, and the faithful stand throughout the lengthy ceremony, except during the actual consecration when the congregation kneels. During baptism in some churches in the East, the god-parents move from the baptismal font to the door of the church and spit into the street as a sign of their rejection of Satan. "Do you renounce Satan?" asks the priest. "I do," answers the god-parent. "Do you spit on Satan?" continues the priest. "I do," responds the god-parent. "Then spit on Satan," directs the priest. At this, the god-parent walks to the door of the Church and spits into the street.

A very distinctive part of the marriage ceremony involves the wearing of crowns, fashioned either from flowers or constructed of metal. The symbolism of the ceremony has to do with the formation of a new kingdom and the beginning of a new dynasty. The celebrant prays that the newly crowned king and queen may enjoy a long and fruitful reign with many loyal subjects.

Perhaps the most apparent dissimilarity between Eastern Rite Christians and Western Rite Christians or, if you will, between Catholic priests and Orthodox priests, concerns celibacy. Among the Christian Churches of the Eastern Rites, including therefore the Catholic Churches of the Eastern Rites, a pastor of a parish is normally a married man. Among Western Rite Catholics, as you well know, married priests are a rarity. Usually, those studying for the priesthood in an Eastern Rite seminary are celibate. Before he becomes an ordained deacon, however, the Eastern Rite seminarian has the option of marrying or remaining celibate. This is the custom today. How did this dissimilarity in discipline arise between the Eastern and Western Christian Churches? For an answer to this question, we must again return to apostolic times and examine the approved practice of those early years of the Church.

We do not know exactly how many of the apostles were married men when they first enrolled among Christ's followers. We do know that they were all Jews and that it was a custom almost to the point of law for Jewish men to marry at an early age. From such a custom, we can hazard a guess that all or nearly all of the apostles were married men. Most of them appear to have been of middle age and engaged in a livelihood or a business. The common opinion is that St. John was not married while all the other apostles were. For St. Peter, the evidence is conclusive since we have the gospel account of Christ curing his mother-in-law.

Regarding the number of married priests and bishops during the first years of the Church, again we are left with little solid evidence, but sufficient to make a safe estimate. Recall the admonition of St. Paul that bishops should be "men of one wife." Paul was not cautioning against a plurality of wives, but noting only that a bishop whose wife had died would not be allowed to remarry. Again, if the apostles were married men when they were chosen for the ministry of Christ, we have a sound basis for assuming that when the time came for them to choose their successors in the small Christian communities scattered throughout the Middle East which they had founded, they would normally follow their Master's practice of choosing men of sound character, upright lives, and well established in their community, rather than untried youths still working as apprentices at various trades. The laying on of hands by the apostles would be the sign to the assembled community of believers that these men were to be their new leaders. In many cases, if not most, this would mean that the "new priest" or the "new bishop" would be a married man with a wife, a family, a business, and a home where the community could assemble for religious services.

Celibacy was recommended in the first centuries, but not demanded of those who were preparing for these offices. For the first ten centuries, a celibate clergy was held in great esteem by Christians of both East and West, although at the same time a married clergy was quite common. The following two centuries saw increasing efforts, especially in the West, to enforce a demand for a celibate clergy. Finally, in 1123 at the First Lateran Council, the sacrament of matrimony for the first time was officially made an impediment in the Western Church to the reception of the sacrament of holy orders. This meant that in the West a married man could not become a priest and continue his married life. Recall that for many centuries the Caerularian dispute with Pope Leo in 1054 had marked the beginning of the separation of the Church in the East from the Church in the West. By the time of the First Lateran Council, neither Church was much influenced by disciplinary changes taking place in the other.

As with the manner of receiving the Holy Eucharist, this definitive change concerning married priests took place over the years following the excommunications exchanged by Michael and Leo when the rift between the two Churches was growing ever wider and deeper. As a consequence, *Western* disciplinary legislation, such as that affecting ordination to the priesthood, was exerting less and less influence on the custom attached to the ordaining of priests in the Christian Churches of the *Eastern* Rites.

In the Eastern Rites of the Catholic as well as the Orthodox Churches, priests do not marry; rather, married men become priests. The proper and allowed sequence of the reception of these two sacraments is matrimony followed by holy orders; hence married men can become priests. If one were allowed to marry after being ordained a priest, then the sequence would be holy orders followed by matrimony. In the event of the death of the wife of a married pastor, he is not allowed to marry again since this would be a case of a priest marrying. Freedom for a widowed pastor to remarry is a much discussed subject finding favor today among many Orthodox.

Monks of the Eastern Rite Churches do not marry. It is a long-standing custom that the bishops of the Eastern Rite Churches are chosen from celibate monks.

Today, married Western Rite Catholic priests in good standing in the Catholic Church are not entirely known, though they are few. The account of the married Lutheran minister Rudolph Goethe, who was received into the Catholic Church and ordained to the priesthood while retaining his marital status, is a matter of public record. Undoubtedly, others, less well publicized, have followed Father Goethe into the Catholic Church and into the priesthood while continuing to live as married men with their wives and families.

The prohibition regarding a married clergy is not a divine positive law; that is, it does not hold the same position in the plan of redemption of the Church as does any of the Ten Commandments. It is a Church law, akin to the laws governing the reception of the Eucharist or the Eucharistic fast. Just as the Church has altered the law respecting the Eucharistic fast, so she can change and has at times changed the laws concerning married clergy.

CHAPTER 8

Promoting Oneness

We began our account of the origins of the Eastern Rites by inviting the reader to attend an Eastern Rite liturgy in any Eastern Rite *Catholic* church. Now, having examined not only the origins of the Eastern Rites but also the origins of the split between the Church at Rome and the Church at Constantinople which gave rise to the Eastern Rite *Orthodox* Churches, we invite, nay along with the fathers and bishops gathered at Vatican II, we encourage Catholics to attend the Divine Liturgy in an Eastern Rite *Orthodox* church:

> Although these Churches are separated from us, they possess true sacraments, above all—by apostolic succession—the priesthood and the Eucharist, whereby they are still joined to us in a very close relationship. Therefore, given suitable circumstances and the approval of Church authority, some worship in common is not merely possible but is recommended.[25]

This encouragement and recommendation carries with it for Catholics a caution:

> As for common worship, however, it may not be regarded as a means to be used indiscriminately for the restoration of unity among Christians. Such worship depends chiefly on two principles: it should signify the unity of the Church; it should provide a sharing in the means of grace. The fact that it should signify unity generally rules out common

worship. Yet the gaining of a needed grace sometimes commends it.[26]

Through the word "indiscriminately," the Bishops at Vatican II in this *Decree on Ecumenism* left the door open to "discriminate" use of shared worship as a means of restoring unity.

In an effort to clarify some of the ambiguities found in the *Decree on Ecumenism*, on May 14, 1967, three years after its promulgation, the Secretariat for Promoting Christian Unity published at Rome a document encumbered with the lengthy title *The Directory for the Application of the Decisions of the Second Ecumenical Council of the Vatican Concerning Ecumenical Matters*. On April 28, 1967, in an audience granted to the Secretariat for Promoting Christian Unity, Pope Paul VI approved this document, now commonly known as *The Directory*, confirmed it by his authority, and ordered that it be published, anything to the contrary notwithstanding. *The Directory* was signed by Jan Willebrands, titular bishop of Mauriana and secretary to the Holy Father, after which it was given to Augustin Cardinal Bea, president of the Secretariat for Promoting Christian Unity.

Regarding the always delicate subject of sharing in liturgical worship, *The Directory* spells out specific directives for Catholics on the necessity of observing Orthodox usages:

> Since practice differs between Catholics and other Eastern Christians in the matter of frequent Communion, confession before Communion and the Eucharistic fast, care must be taken to avoid scandal and suspicion among the Orthodox created by Catholics not following the Orthodox usage. A Catholic who legitimately communicates with the Orthodox in the cases envisaged here must observe the Orthodox discipline as much as he can.[27]

Two paragraphs later, *The Directory* cites a striking reversal of the position formerly held by the Catholic Church regarding a Catholic's participation at an Orthodox liturgy on a Sunday or holy day of obligation:

A Catholic who occasionally for reasons set out below attends the Holy Liturgy (Mass) on a Sunday or a holy day of obligation in an Orthodox Church is not then bound to assist at Mass in a Catholic Church. It is likewise a good thing if on such days Catholics who for just reasons cannot go to Mass in their own Church attend the Holy Liturgy of their separated Oriental brethren, if this is possible.[28]

Finally, *The Directory* offers specific reasons for participating in an Orthodox liturgy and clarifies the extent to which a Catholic may share in the worship:

Catholics may be allowed to attend Orthodox liturgical services if they have reasonable grounds, e.g. arising out of a public office or function, blood relationships, friendships, a desire to be better informed, etc. In such cases there is nothing against their taking part in the common responses, hymns, and actions of the Church in which they are guests. Receiving Holy Communion, however, will be governed by what is laid down above in nn. 42 and 44. Because of the close communion referred to earlier, local Ordinaries can give permission for a Catholic to read lessons at a liturgical service, if invited.[29]

In no. 42 and no. 44 of *The Directory*, the Catholic is advised to seek and obtain the permission of the Orthodox pastor before presenting himself to receive the Eucharist in an Orthodox church.

OBSTACLES TO THE RECOVERY OF ONENESS

As the Catholic traditionally looks at the situation, the Orthodox Churches began in schism by rejecting the supreme governing authority of the Bishop of Rome, the Vicar of Christ, the successor of St. Peter, the supreme ruler of the universal Church. However, from the time of Michael Caerularius to the present, the Catholic seems to find the Orthodox Churches subscribing to heresies or teachings which the Catholic would call heretical in rejecting papal infallibility, primacy of jurisdiction of the Bishop of Rome in the entire Christian world, the doctrine of the Immaculate Conception, the doctrine of purgatory.

The author's *Brothers East and West* presents the views of selected Orthodox on some problems of reunion. The question "What separates us now?" was put to Miss Selma Fayad, officer of the *Syndesmos* group in Beirut, Lebanon. She responded:

I really do not know. The *"Filioque,"* the primacy of the Bishop of Rome, Papal Infallibility, all historically have figured in the separation; but though they remain problems, still I don't think they are major obstacles to union today. More divisive than these doctrinal differences is the "trench" that we have succeeded in digging around ourselves over the centuries. We seem to be two different civilizations. We are two worlds separated from one another in fact, but not so much any more by doctrinal differences.[30]

For Mitri Tarik, another *Syndesmos* officer, the so-called differences in doctrine "are minor; the real differences are not in actual doctrine, but rather in the cultural approach to the living out of one's Faith."[31]

Dr. Panayotis Christou, Greek Orthodox ecumenist at the Ecumenical Center of Tantur near Bethlehem, speaks in the same vein: "The doctrinal differences which separate Catholics from Orthodox today are not very many nor very serious. In reality, they never were much more serious in the past than they are today."[32]

While doctrinal differences seem to be disappearing, many non-doctrinal differences are growing in importance. "Westernization" or "Latinization" or "hybridization" still remains a factor to be considered when reunion is being discussed. Among ecumenists in the two Churches the doctrinal differences with one or two exceptions are rarely brought up for examination as obstacles to reunion. Anti-reunion propagandists can surely be expected in the future to point to the absence of icon screens in many Eastern Rite Catholic churches as evidence of the slow but inevitable process of westernization that is taking place. The presence of confessional boxes in Eastern Rite Catholic churches as well as the Stations of the Cross will offer ammunition to be used against those who vainly insist that to be one with the Catholic Church the Orthodox will not have to give up any of her ancient customs.

Among the non-doctrinal obstacles to oneness between Orthodox and Catholics, one can single out the self-isolation that the two Churches have built up over the centuries, resulting today in a reluctance to pray together, a reluctance to worship together. Too, the unsettled condition of theology in the Catholic Church coupled with the underdeveloped condition of theology in the Orthodox Churches makes it difficult to point out "What the Church teaches" as distinguished from "What the theologians are teaching." Among the Orthodox, the disproportionate influence of the monks in the process of forming the *pleroma* leads to an ultra-conservative position of Orthodox theologians. The misunder-

standing of many of the faithful, both Catholic and
Orthodox, of infallibility, especially of the *Church*
as distinct from infallibility of the *pope,* again con-
tributes in great measure to the present stalemate.
Nor when speaking of non-doctrinal obstacles should
we omit the clumsy and involved wording of the
teaching on infallibility as it is found in Vatican I.

Remedies for overcoming many of these obstacles
are at hand. In general, both Churches are now
putting the accent on the positive, searching out
areas of agreement rather than focusing their atten-
tion constantly on points where the two Churches
disagree.

Vatican II has led the way in emphasizing self-
government for the Eastern Rite Churches and in
adding the teaching of collegiality to the teaching
of Vatican I on the "monarchical" structure of government in the Church of Christ:

> From the earliest times, moreover, the Eastern Churches
> followed their own disciplines, sanctioned by the holy
> Fathers, by synods, even ecumenical Councils. Far from
> being an obstacle to the Church's unity, such diversity of
> customs and observances only add to her comeliness, and
> contributes greatly to carrying out her mission. . . . To
> remove any shadow of doubt, then, this sacred Synod
> solemnly declares that the Churches of the East, while
> keeping in mind the necessary unity of the whole Church,
> have the power to govern themselves according to their
> own disciplines, since they are better suited to the tem-
> perament of their faithful and better adapted to foster the
> good of souls. Although it has not always been honored,
> the strict observance of this traditional principle is among
> the prerequisites for any restoration of unity.[33]

With genuine sympathy for the rights of those
belonging to the various rites in the Church of
Christ and declaring without any hesitation that

the synod favors strongly self-government as a sacred duty, the bishops at Vatican II said:

> This sacred Synod, therefore, not only honors this ecclesi-
> astical and spiritual heritage with merited esteem and
> rightful praise, but also unhesitatingly looks upon it as
> the heritage of Christ's universal Church. For this reason,
> it solemnly declares that the Churches of the East, as much
> as those of the West, fully enjoy the right and are in duty
> bound, to rule themselves. Each should do so according
> to its proper and individual procedures, inasmuch as prac-
> tices sanctioned by a noble antiquity harmonize better
> with the customs of the faithful and are seen as more
> likely to foster the good of souls.[34]

Will Catholics be able to temper the strong
monarchical stand taken in Vatican I regarding the
Bishop of Rome with the stand taken for collegiality
in Vatican II? How long will it take for the phrase
"first among equals" to stand side by side or even
displace the phrase "first among un-equals"? Will
primacy of honor ever catch up with *primacy of
jurisdiction* when describing the role of the Bishop
of Rome in the government of the Church of Christ?
Only time will yield the answers to these and similar
questions that continue to bother ecumenists.

PROSPECTS OF ONENESS

The popes have insisted perseveringly that the
Eastern Rites be preserved in their purity. To effect
a full union of Catholic and Orthodox Churches, the
latter will not be obliged to remove their icon screens
or don Western vestments. They will not be re-
quired to ban their married clergy or change their
method of receiving the Eucharist. Their liturgical
language as their liturgical calendar will remain as
they are. In like manner, the Catholic Church will

not be forced to adopt any or all of the Eastern Rite customs. Certain concessions will be made without a doubt, but these will be made voluntarily rather than under duress or as a prerequisite for reunion.

That all Christians may be at one with one another is the prayer of Christ. That the community of believers, whether of Eastern or Western Rite, whether Catholic or non-Catholic, may become one effective instrument for spreading the Good News of the Risen Christ to men of all ages and all nations . . . this is the prayer of Christ today.

There is no better way to bring this brief study to a close than to quote once more from the *Guidelines for Ecumenics* for the Orthodox:

We recall Jesus asking the Father . . . "that they may be one as we are one" (Jn. 17:2). And as it is not given to us fully to know the nature of that inner one-ness of Father and Son, so we may not fully comprehend the nature of the Church's inner one-ness. As a Russian layman expressed it more than a century ago, perhaps we are bound together "by ties which God has not yet willed to reveal to us."[35]

Notes

1. *Eastern Branches of the Catholic Church: Six Studies of the Oriental Rites,* compiled by the Liturgical Arts Society, introduction by Donald Attwater (New York: Longmans, Green, and Co., 1938), p. ix.

2. Walter M. Abbott, S.J., ed. *The Documents of Vatican II* (New York: America Press, 1966), p. 376.

3. See Edward Finn, S.J., *Brothers East and West* (Collegeville, Minn.: The Liturgical Press, 1975), pp. 25–28.

4. Abbott, p. 173.

5. *Ibid.,* p. 374.

6. *A Catholic Dictionary* (New York: Macmillan Co., 1949), p. 388.

7. *The Official Catholic Directory* (New York: P. J. Kenedy & Sons, 1976), p. 3.

8. *The New Catholic Dictionary* (New York: Gilmary Society, 1929), p. 733.

9. See Francis Dvornik, *Byzantium and the Roman Primacy* (New York: Fordham University Press, 1966), pp. 27–40.

10. See Timothy Ware, *The Orthodox Church* (Baltimore: Penguin Books, Inc., 1965), p. 55.

11. *Ibid.,* p. 57.

12. Abbott, p. 345.

13. Ware, p. 55.

14. *Ibid.,* p. 35.

15. *A New Catechism* (New York: Seabury Press, Inc., 1969), pp. 348ff.

16. Ware, p. 36.

17. *Diakonia,* vol. 7, no. 4 (New York: John XXIII Center), p. 396.

18. Abbott, p. 356.

19. Leonidas Contos, *Guidelines for the Orthodox in Ecumenical Relations* (New York: Standing Conference of Canonical Orthodox Bishops in America, 1966), p. 3.

20. John Meyendorff, *The Orthodox Church* (New York: Pantheon Books, Inc., 1960), pp. 145ff.

21. See Helene Iswolsky, *Christ in Russia* (Milwaukee: Bruce Publishing Co., 1960), pp. 78ff.

22. "U.S., Russians, and Autocephality," *One in Christ* 1, no. 3 (1965), p. 277.

23. Abbott, p. 345.

24. Louis J. Puhl, S.J., *The Spiritual Exercises of St. Ignatius* (Chicago: Loyola University Press, 1951), pp. 157ff.

25. Abbott, p. 359.

26. *Ibid.,* p. 352.

27. *The Directory on Ecumenical Matters* (Washington: United States Catholic Conference, 1967), no. 45.

28. *Ibid.,* no. 47.

29. *Ibid.,* no. 50.

30. Finn, pp. 63–64.

31. *Ibid.,* p. 64.

32. *Ibid.,* p. 67.

33. Abbott, pp. 359–60.

34. *Ibid.,* p. 376.

35. Contos, p. 3.

The AUTHOR

Fr. Edward E. Finn, S.J., currently the acting assistant chairman of the theology department at Marquette University and an associate professor emeritus of that department, has long been a scholar of the various rites of the universal Church as well as the Orthodox Churches of Eastern Christendom. See also his *Brothers East and West* published in 1975 by The Liturgical Press. Father Finn has also published articles on the rites of the Church in several journals and in the *New Catholic Encyclopedia*. He holds A.B., M.A., Ph.L., and S.T.L. degrees from St. Louis University.

Diagrams by John Maddigan, S.J.

Cover photo of the Lion's Gate, Jerusalem, by Hugh Witzmann, O.S.B.